A Survival Guide

FOR

Project Managers

Second Edition

A Survival Guide

FOR

Project Managers

Second Edition

James Taylor

ᴬMACOM

American Management Association

New York • Atlanta • Brussels • Chicago • Mexico City • San Francisco
Shanghai • Tokyo • Toronto • Washington, D.C.

This publication is designed to provide accurate and authoritative information in regard to the subject matter covered. It is sold with the understanding that the publisher is not engaged in rendering legal, accounting, or other professional service. If legal advice or other expert assistance is required, the services of a competent professional person should be sought.

"PMI" and the PMI logo are service and trademarks registered in the United States and other nations; "PMP" and the PMP logo are certification marks registered in the United States and other nations; "PMBOK," "PM Network," and "PMI Today" are trademarks registered in the United States and other nations; and "Project Management Journal" and "Building professionalism in project management" are trademarks of the Project Management Institute, Inc.

Library of Congress Cataloging-in-Publication Data

Taylor, James
    A survival guide for project managers / James Taylor.—2nd ed.
      p. cm.
    Includes bibliographical references and index.
    ISBN-10: 0-8144-0877-X
    ISBN-13: 978-0-8144-0877-3
    1. Project management. I. Title.

  HD69 .P75T39 2006
  658.4' 04—dc22   2005030962

Printing Hole Number

10 9 8 7 6 5 4 3 2 1

Contents

A Survival Guide

FOR

Project
Managers

Second Edition

Human Skills and Technical Tools

Introduction to Part One

Project management is a specialized approach to managing today's business, yet most project managers are people who have never had any training, other than on-the-job training, about the art and science of project management. So mistakes are perpetuated, and a concept that came into being specifically to solve the problems of inefficient management itself becomes just another inefficient management concept.

This book is intended to provide the new project managers or project team members with a fundamental understanding of project management essentials. These essentials are explained and discussed in Part One. Part Two discusses the phases of a project's life, and how and when to apply the skill sets of Part One. With a solid base of knowledge about the technical and human tools of project management, and when and how to use them, you can then confidently manage a project to successful conclusion.

What is Project Management?

Project management is the art and science of managing relatively short-term efforts having finite beginning and ending points, usually with a specific budget, and with customer-specified performance criteria. "Short-term" in the context of project duration is dependent upon the industry. For example, in the construction industry, a house might be built in three months while a hospital might take two years. In the aerospace industry, a new airplane might take eight to ten years to design and build. In the Department of Defense's training environment, it is usual practice to award a contract for fifteen years for a contractor to manage, operate, and maintain a training complex. The longer and more complex a project is, the more it will benefit from the application of project management tools.

The concept of project management is relatively new. It was in the 1950s that a conscious effort was made to devise specialized tools for managing the complex weapon systems being built for the Department of Defense. These tools are in widespread use today in all industries, public and private. The tools of project management make it a science. However, there is much, much more to managing projects than just applying analytical tools to help monitor, track, and control them. The bigger problems for project managers are those associated with the human element: conflict resolution, team building, coaching, mentoring, and negotiating. The application of the skills necessary to cope with this element constitutes the art part of project management.

Why Project Management?

The last forty years have witnessed a rapid and staggering change in technology and global competition. With these changes, the nature of business has become more complex and more dynamic. Companies have become more diverse in the products or services they offer, and increasing, or even maintaining, market share has become more competitive. In his book on project management, Harold Kerzner lists five questions:[1]

1. Are the jobs complex?
2. Are there dynamic environmental considerations?
3. Are the constraints tight?
4. Are there several activities to be integrated?
5. Are there several functional boundaries to be crossed?

If the answer to any of these questions is yes, there may be a need for some form of formalized project management. When a company decides to approach its business from a project management perspective, the project manager is going to need two distinct classes of skills: technical, which deals with monitoring, tracking, and controlling a project, and human or relational skills, which deals with the problems that invariably arise from the interaction of people with the project.

Technical Skill Requirements

Project managers do not have to be specialists in the project's technology. Some authorities indeed argue that project managers should be generalists because they thus have a better chance of understanding the project from a holistic point of reference. The more complex a project is—that is, the more subsystems to be integrated, the more tasks to be accomplished, the more technically challenging the components—the better suited a generalist will be as the project manager. Regardless of the project manager's level of technical expertise, this person must have a good understanding of and facility using several tools designed specifically for monitoring, tracking, and controlling the project. These tools are explained in Part One.

The increase in global competition and the extraordinary growth in information technology have created other problems for project managers—problems that have more to do with human relations than with the technical skills.

Management Skill Requirements

There is much more demand on the project manager's interpersonal and negotiating skills today than there was even twenty years ago. The traditional, vertical organizational hierarchy, which has been the model for all organizational structures since it was invented by the early Roman army until the mid-1900s, is too slow and inflexible to respond to today's competitive challenges, and information technology is being used, among other things, to disperse the workforce from centralized and expensive office complexes to smaller telecommuting sites or to home offices.

Other attempts to cut costs include the establishment of cross-functional teams to use the resources of the company better, flattening the organization to reduce management levels and expedite decision making and communication, and using fewer but better-trained people.

All of these efforts at making the company more efficient and cost-effective are precisely the areas that project management was developed to handle. But with the relatively recent emphasis upon such things as cross-functional teams, flat organizational structures, increasing diversity in the employee ranks, and empowerment of the employees, project managers have to be more than just technical managers; they have to be team builders, mentors, and negotiators as well. These and other skills are discussed in Part One.

It is important to understand the technical and management tools needed for project management, but without the knowledge of when and how to apply them, the skills are useless. Part Two explores the phases of a project's life cycle, and demonstrates how the tools are applied in each of the phases.

This brings us to the objective of this book: to provide a balance between the technical and management skills required, and the knowledge of how and when to apply them.

This book is written to be consistent with the standards and principles of the Project Management Institute (PMI®) and the Project Management Body of Knowledge (PMBOK®). PMI® and PMBOK® are discussed in Chapter 1 in the discussion on project management skills and the problems of project management.

Note

1. Harold Kerzner, *Project Management; A Systems Approach to Planning, Scheduling, and Controlling*. 8th ed. (New York: Wiley, 2003).

The Human Skills

CHAPTER 1

Project Management Skills

Today, inspiration, though still necessary,
is no longer enough for the manager.

—Peter Guest
How to Manage Large Multidisciplinary Engineering Groups

Managing projects in today's environment of large, complex projects, several subcontractors working on the same project, matrixed or cross-functional teams, and multicultural organizations has radically changed the way we manage and, consequently, the skills required of project managers.

Not too many years ago, it was thought that as long as a person had strong technical skills and demonstrated a certain amount of aggressiveness and enthusiasm, and had worked on several project teams for experience, he could be given the role of a project manager. Notice that I didn't say that one of the characteristics was the ability to get along with other people. Although that was a definite plus, it really wasn't considered a necessary quality to successfully manage a project. Notice also that I referred to the project manager as "he." There weren't significant numbers of women in project management until about 1985.

This chapter discusses the evolution of project management and the major skills of the most successful project managers.

Project Management as a Career Path

Traditionally, the career paths leading to the top corporate positions were usually through finance or marketing. Today, an increasing number of organizations are adopting project management concepts as a way to manage their businesses. Project management is now recognized as a legitimate career path, and many organizations are choosing their top corporate officers from the project manager ranks. It really is not surprising that a highly trained and experienced project manager would make a good top executive, because running a large, complex project is like running a small company; the project manager needs to have broad experience in all aspects of an organization.

The organizations that are adopting the project management concept to manage their businesses are also going to great lengths to ensure that their project managers are highly trained. Companies such as AT&T, IBM, Bell South, and Citibank are sending project managers through rigorous training courses to prepare them for certification as a project management professional (PMP®).

The Project Management Institute (PMI®) is the certifying body that bestows the PMP® certification. (PMI® also offers a credential as a certified associate in project management for project team members and entry-level project managers, as well as qualified undergraduate and graduate students, to recognize that they are on the path to project management.) This organization was begun in 1969 by a group of concerned managers to help improve the quality of project management work. Now there are more than 170,000 certified project managers worldwide. The PMI® membership of professional project managers has identified a body of knowledge, known as the Project Management Body of Knowledge (PM-BOK®), which represents the knowledge areas that a project manager needs to master before becoming a certified project management professional(-PMP®).[1] The following list is taken from the most current *PMBOK® Guide* (2004):

- Project Integration Management (Project charter, project plan development, execution, and change control)

- Project Scope Management (Scope definition and planning)
- Project Time Management (Time in the sense of duration estimation, schedule control, and task interdependencies)
- Project Cost Management (Resource planning, cost estimating, cost budgeting, and cost control)
- Project Quality Management (Quality planning, quality assurance, quality control)
- Project Human Resources Management (Organizational planning, staff acquisition, and team development)
- Project Communications Management (Planning, information distribution, project progress reporting, and other administrative requirements)
- Project Risk Management (Risk identification, risk quantification, risk control)
- Project Procurement Management (Solicitation, source selection, contracts and contract management)

The point is that project management has become a serious career field, and one in which many large companies are willing to invest heavily in having a trained, professional project manager corps. Additional information about PMI® and the project management certification process can be obtained by contacting PMI® at:

Project Management Institute
Four Campus Boulevard
Newtown Square, Pennsylvania 19073-3299
www.pmi.org

Project Management Skills

Project managers can no longer depend upon their positions or their initiative or their enthusiasm to accomplish the goal of a project successfully. Because most projects are managed from a matrix organization (see Chapter 10 for a discussion of various organizational forms), project managers have no functional control or authority over the project team members. Consequently, the project manager must have strong interpersonal skills to negotiate for the resources needed for the team, and then he or she must motivate and lead the team throughout the life of the project as well as in technical and organizational skills.

Several years ago, Barry Posner, a professor of organizational behavior and managing partner of the Executive Development Center, Leavey School of Business and Administration, Santa Clara University, wrote a report on the problems of project management and the skills needed to cope with them.[2] Posner's report is the basis for his now famous model for training project managers. As of 2005, he has presented this model worldwide—to more than 1 million people. Although conducted nearly twenty years ago, his study is as relevant and instructive as when it was first done.

Prior to Posner's study, there were essentially two views about the skills needed to run projects successfully. One school of thought held that the successful project manager needed to have a set of personal characteristics, such as aggressiveness, versatility, and decisiveness, to be able to accomplish the goals of a project successfully. On the other hand, some scholars thought that it would be too difficult to find people possessing all these requisite characteristics. Therefore, they argued that the emphasis should be on determining just the critical problems of a typical project and then finding people with skills that fit the critical problems. Posner found, however, that these two schools of thought really were not two different approaches but actually "two sides of the same coin."

Posner surveyed experienced project managers from across the United States. The project managers were from various backgrounds and managed all types and sizes of projects. He asked the following two opened-ended questions in his survey:

1. What factors or variables are most likely to cause you problems in managing a project?
2. What personal characteristics, traits, or skills make for above-average project managers? What specific behaviors,

techniques, or strategies do above-average project managers use (or use better than their peers)?

The responders to the survey provided a large number of statements about the problems of project management, all of which fell into one of eight categories. The list of eight project management problems, in the order of most often to the least often occurring problem, are shown in Exhibit 1-1. Not surprisingly, the most often mentioned problem is the lack of adequate resources and the next most often mentioned problem is the setting of unrealistic schedules.

Inadequate resources occur for many reasons. On the surface, the most obvious reason is that organizations are forced into having to do more with less in order to be competitive. Although that can be a contributing factor, in reality, it is more likely that inadequate resources occur because of poor planning or inefficient usage of available resources. Whatever the reason, it is no less a problem to the project manager who is suddenly in the position of having to accomplish a project's goals without a staff of sufficient size or qualification to do it.

Unrealistic deadlines occur all too often. Usually these are deadlines imposed by the organization because it is reactively responding to a need or because it is promising earlier delivery in a bid to make the company appear more attractive competitively. Again, the project manager is stuck with the problem of accomplishing the project's goals sooner than is reasonable or, in many cases, possible.

Exhibit 1-1. Problems most often encountered in project management.

1. Inadequate Resources
2. Unrealistic Schedules
3. Unclear Goals and Senior Executive Direction
4. Uncommitted Team Members
5. Inadequate Planning
6. Communication Breakdowns
7. Goal and Resource Changes
8. Interdepartmental Conflicts

The third of these problems, unclear goals and objectives, is to my mind the biggest problem encountered in project management. The most difficult task often is simply determining what the customer wants. Many customers themselves do not know what they want, which usually results in several expensive false starts.

The second question Posner asked relative to what skills make a difference in successfully managing a project yielded an even greater number of statements from the responders. All these statements have been condensed into six major categories and are shown in Exhibit 1-2. Note that five of the six categories listed deal with interpersonal skills. This fact points out exactly why initiative or organizational position alone is no longer sufficient for successful project management. The majority of project problems encountered by project managers are not technical but interpersonal problems.

The first essential skill is the ability to communicate. This skill is important in any endeavor but is absolutely crucial in project management. It has been estimated that project managers spend 90 percent of their time just communicating: with the project team, the customer, functional managers, and upper management.

Exhibit 1-2. Skills needed to be a successful project manager.

1. Communication Skills	4. Leadership Skills
Listening	Sets Example
Persuading	Energetic
2. Organizational Skills	Vision (sees the big picture)
Planning	Delegates
Goal Setting	Positive Attitude
Analyzing	5. Coping Skills
3. Team-Building Skills	Flexibility
Empathy	Creativity
Motivation	Patience
Esprit de Corps	Persistence
Creativity	6. Technological Skills
	Experience
	Project Knowledge

One of the subcategories under communication skills in Exhibit 1-2 is "persuading." Although persuading can be loosely interpreted to mean negotiating, I prefer the word *negotiating* because it is a stronger term. Project managers spend a large portion of their time negotiating for resources or equipment or other support, and if they do not have strong negotiating skills, their chances of being successful project managers are greatly reduced.

One other important point of interest in Exhibit 1-2 is that the category of "technical skills" is listed last. Although technical expertise is important, project managers do not need to be expert in the project's technical area. In fact, it is better that the project manager be a generalist rather than an expert. The reason is that experts tend to be very narrow in their views. Experts leading a project are less likely to consider any other view than their own. The tendency is for experts to believe their solution is the right one, and therefore the only choice. A generalist, on the other hand, is far more open to the views and suggestions of the team members. On balance, the results of projects led by a generalist tend to yield much better deliverables than a comparable project led by an expert.

Posner related the results of the two survey questions to show that they are not really mutually exclusive. Exhibit 1-3 shows how the skills and problems of project management are related to each other.

Posner's study succinctly states and categorizes the requisite project management skills needed to manage a project successfully. But it is worthwhile looking at the same subject from a slightly different perspective. That is, by taking the personal skills from Posner and the areas of knowledge required by PMI® for its PMP® certification, we can see that today's project manager really does need to be a generalist and, more than that, a generalist with extraordinary interpersonal skills.

Successful project managers need qualifications in the following four categories:

1. Personal characteristics
2. Behavioral skills

Exhibit 1-3. The relationship of problem management skills and problems.

Communication	Communication breakdowns
Organizational	Inadequate planning, insufficient resources
Team Building	Uncommitted team members, weak interdepartmental interaction and support
Leadership	Unclear goals and senior executive direction, interpersonal conflicts
Coping	Handling changes
Technical	Meeting unrealistic schedules

Source: Reprinted from Jack R. Merredith and Samuel J. Mantel, Jr., *Project Management: A Managerial Approach* (New York: John Wiley & Sons, Inc., 1985, 1989, and 1995). Copyright © 1985, 1989, and 1995 John Wiley & Sons. Reprinted by permission of John Wiley & Sons, Inc.

3. Business skills
4. Technical skills

The personal characteristics include a wide variety of competencies and innate personal abilities and skills, including the following:

- Flexibility
- Leadership
- Communication
- Disciplined
- Organized
- Decisiveness
- Negotiation

The behavioral skills in some cases overlap with the personal characteristics required. These skills include those dealing with how a person relates to others. In other words, having good communication skills means knowing how to be articulate and how to present information. However, a lack of behavioral skills that make a person an active listener would render the communication skills less effective.

Business skills are a combination of technical and interpersonal skills. The technical side deals with organizational skills, marketing, business development, strategic planning, cash flow, and profit and loss. The interpersonal skills for this category are those that help the person teach or mentor subordinates so that they are better project and company members.

Summary

Project management has become a recognized career path in today's business environment. With more and more companies turning to project management as a better way of managing their businesses, they are also finding that their project managers need more training.

Not long ago, a project manager was chosen because of his, and occasionally her, technical expertise and general enthusiasm or aggressiveness. Those days are gone forever. Today's project manager has to be a generalist with strong interpersonal skills.

This chapter has discussed these skills as a precursor to the following chapters, which address these critical skills, both technical and interpersonal, in greater detail.

CHAPTER 2

Communication Skills

Good, the more communicated, more abundant grows.

—JOHN MILTON
(1608–1674)
Paradise Lost

No other ability is more valuable to a person, project manager or otherwise, than the ability to communicate effectively with other people. We communicate almost constantly and have done so all our lives. Why, then, should we be concerned about communicating if it is something we practice daily? The fact is that many of us do not communicate well, and even those of us who do can always improve our skills.

The word *communicate* comes from the Latin word *communis,* which means "common." The idea is to come together on a common ground of understanding. All means for transferring information, emotions, or thoughts fall within the purview of communication. Therefore, communication includes oral, written, and nonverbal means between two people. Nonverbal communication enters into both oral and written communication. Body language cues in oral communication help to clarify the message; the lack of body language cues in written communication often obscures the message. Communication between machines or between people and machines also occurs, but our principal concern in this chapter is the communication that occurs between two or more persons.

The Project Manager as a Communicator

Although communication skills are important to us all, it is easy to see that some situations require better-developed communication skills than other situations. For instance, effectively communicating in a social setting, albeit important, may not be as critical as effectively communicating during a negotiation session. In a social situation, the inability to communicate effectively would mean that one wouldn't be a popular conversation companion. In a serious negotiation, the inability to communicate could mean the loss of money or business. In other words, although effective communication is desirable in every human endeavor, it is crucial for success in some of them. Project management is one of those endeavors.

Project managers spend most of their time communicating. They hold meetings; report (orally as well as in writing) to the team, customer, or senior management; listen to problems; solve problems; and constantly negotiate with functional managers for resources. Project managers' success depends greatly on their ability to communicate.

In the project management environment, there are four types of communication:

1. Formal written (project charter, status reports)
2. Informal written (project notes, memos)
3. Formal oral (presentations)
4. Informal oral (conversations, team meetings)

In the formal and informal oral communication environments, the listening skills are employed as facilitative or as critical listening or both. The effectiveness with which these three skills of speaking, writing, and listening are used is important to the success of the project and the project manager.

The Project Manager's Problem: Potential Channels of Communication

The project manager must deal with a large number of people: the team, functional managers across the organization, senior management, customers, customers' representatives, vendors, and still others. To put the size of the problem into perspective, consider this: The number of potential channels of communication available relative to the number of people involved can be expressed mathematically:

$$\text{Number of communication channels} = \frac{n(n-1)}{2}$$

For example, if there are four people in a group, the number of channels of communication will be:

$$\text{Number of communication channels} = \frac{4(4-1)}{2} = \frac{12}{2} = 6$$

And for a group of six people:

$$\text{Number of communication channels} = \frac{6(6-1)}{2} = \frac{30}{2} = 15.$$

The potential lines of communication for a group of six people are graphically depicted in Exhibit 2-1.

Even for a relatively small project team of eight people, the number of communication channels will be twenty-eight. For each person added to the communication network, the number of possible communication channels increases geometrically. Relating this concept to the number of people with whom the project manager typically interfaces on any given day, the possible number of communication channels is enormous. Clearly, the project manager's communication role is the most far-reaching one, and one of the most important.

To understand the communication challenge requires that we first look at the general process of communication—that is, the process of sending and receiving a message.

A Communication Model: Sending and Receiving Messages

We often marvel at how the simplest messages can sometimes be received so differently from the way we thought they were trans-

Exhibit 2-1. Channels of communication for a six-member team.

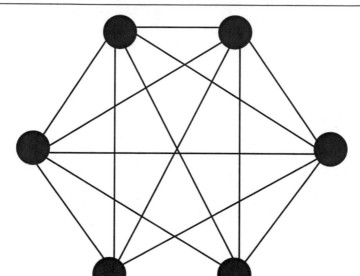

mitted. This phenomenon is the basis for the children's game of Telephone, in which one person starts the process by whispering a message into the ear of his neighbor, and the next person continues the process by whispering the message she thought she heard into the ear of her neighbor. When the last person repeats the message aloud, the ending message seldom resembles the beginning one. This transmutation of messages can be explained using a variation of the Shannon-Weaver model shown in Exhibit 2-2. The Shannon-Weaver model was first published by Claude Shannon in a Bell System technical journal and later included in a work coauthored with Warren Weaver.[1] (Their model did not include the feedback loop.)

From the exhibit, you can see that there are five parts involved in the communication process: (1) the messenger or message generator, (2) the message itself, (3) the channel or medium of transmittal, (4) the receiver, and (5) feedback. I include feedback in this process because successful communication occurs when the message is understood and accomplishes its purpose, and this can be known only through feedback from the intended message receiver.

Exhibit 2-2. A communication model.

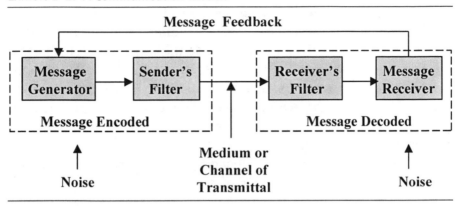

In addition to these five communication components, there is out-side noise in the form of distractions and other disturbances inter-posing themselves into the message channel.

Why Messages Go Astray

Each of us is a message generator or receiver, depending on whether we are sending a message or receiving it. When a message generator attempts to communicate with another person, she for-mulates the message in her mind. As this message is formulated, it is filtered with preconceptions about the intended receiver's abil-ity to understand it. Sometimes the preconception is wrong, result-ing in the transmitted message being either too simple or too complex. Perhaps the language used is vague because of an as-sumed higher level of understanding or experience than exists. Regardless, the message is filtered through the generator's own ex-periences and background before it is put into the communication channel, and because of that, the message is already subject to misinterpretation.

The message generator also packages the message with differ-ent facial expressions—a smile perhaps—or other body and voice tones that shade the message. Consider the difference in a message that is conciliatory on paper from the same message delivered verbally with a sneer and a sarcastic tone. This encoding of the message with distinctive body and voice characteristics has a significant bearing on how the message is received.

The receiver of the message has a similar set of filters as the sender. First, the receiver has to decode the body and voice packaging of the message and assess whether there are hidden meanings in the sender's words. Then the receiver filters the message through his own experiences and background to determine whether the message is on a common ground of understanding with the sender.

On top of all the encoding, decoding, and filtering that is done by both the sender and receiver of a message, there is added yet another complication: noise—that is, any distraction that is constantly at work during an exchange of messages. This distraction includes not only actual noise, such as loud talking, banging doors, and outside traffic, but also irritating habits of the sender or receiver, such as mumbling, poor grammar, incomplete sentences, or biased or vulgar language. If the message is written, noise could be in the form of poor handwriting or poor spelling.

It is not hard to understand why messages go astray. The question is: What can be done to improve the process? To improve the process requires an understanding of the five processes of verbal communication.

The Five Processes of Verbal Communication

Verbal communications—those dealing with words, whether orally transmitted or written—encompass the following five processes:

1. Speaking
2. Writing
3. Reading
4. Listening
5. Thinking

The three processes that most clearly affect the project manager's ability to communicate and to function in the project management role are speaking, writing, and listening skills. This chapter addresses each of these processes in order and points out the problems encountered in each, along with some suggestions about how to improve them. Developing critical reading and thinking skills is also important, but these skills are beyond the scope of this book.

Developing Speaking Skills

If a professional project manager is asked to describe what a project manager does, the answer most often given is, "I get things done." If you are having trouble getting things done, even though you're using all the tools and techniques described in this book, chances are that you are having a communications problem.

Since project managers must constantly communicate with a variety of audiences, and most of the communication is oral, the place to start is in the improvement of their speaking and presentation skills.

Taking Stock

We usually are not our best sources for objective criticism, but it is beneficial to assess our communication strengths and weaknesses periodically. Some of the questions we need to ask, with as objective a view as possible, include the following:

- How clear is my speaking voice?
- Do I mumble or slur my words?
- Am I careful about the choice of my words? Do I use slang excessively, or profanity? Do I ever use racial or sexually biased language?
- Do I use correct grammar?

Many people will be surprised at the number of bad habits they have because we don't often take stock of our shortcomings.

After self-assessment, it is beneficial to ask someone close—a spouse, parent, or sibling—to provide a similar assessment. Using several data points, you can develop and implement a plan for improving your communication skills. Exhibit 2-3 illustrates this process.

The project manager is required to communicate on a one-to-one basis as well as in groups and to groups. Presentation skills are basic skill requirements that can be used in each of these scenarios, and they can be learned with a little guidance and practice. The next section discusses presentation skills with the view that they are equally applicable to the one-to-one situation as well as to small or large groups.

Developing Presentation Skills

Project managers regularly communicate on a one-to-one basis, as well as in groups and to groups. Presentation skills are basic skill requirements that can be used in each of these settings, and they can be learned with a little guidance and practice.

Some of the steps you need to take to present information include the following:

1. *Prepare content.* Determine what it is you need to relay to your team.
2. *Determine how to deliver the content in the best way possible.* This may require that you learn new skills such as how to use PowerPoint or other presentation programs.
3. *Prepare for the actual event.* If you will be presenting in per-

Exhibit 2-3. Process for communication assessment, plan preparation, and implementation.

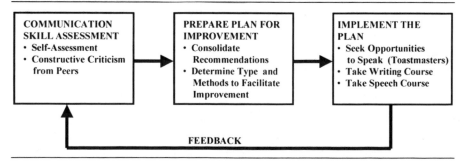

son at a meeting, your preparation will be different than, say, a written presentation. Most project information is relayed in meetings. You may want to prepare an agenda, book a room, send out premeeting materials, make sure everything you need to make the presentation is in the room, and so forth.

The more you prepare for a presentation, the better it will go. Exhibit 2-4 presents a checklist for ensuring that the presentation is as good as you can make it.

Most people have difficulty presenting because getting in front of a group makes them nervous. There is no doubt that making a presentation before a group is harder than talking to one or two people. However, project management is a profession that requires speaking both one-to-one and to groups. The effort to break

Exhibit 2-4. Checklist for preparing a presentation.

1. Determine the goals of the presentation.
2. Consider a case- or problem-centered approach.
3. Identify a way of starting the presentation that will grab the audience.
4. Make an outline.
5. Structure the session in a logical way.
6. Include divergent viewpoints or issues.
7. Break the material into short sections to facilitate questions and discussion.
8. Create transition slides to help the audience move from one section or point to the next.
9. Build in variety, surprise, or changes of pace.
10. Don't overwhelm the audience with information—make each slide comprehensible, simple, and tied with a thread throughout the presentation.
11. Prepare for unexpected events and needed changes.
12. Identify and make arrangements for audiovisuals and other resources.
13. Test the presentation equipment before the audience arrives.
14. Monitor the time.
15. Develop a strong conclusion related to the presentation content.

this pattern of not trying will provide the impetus to improve, and improving your ability to speak before a group has the added benefit of increasing your overall confidence and capability to deal one-to-one. These misconceptions about making presentations or speaking while in a group create an enormous amount of apprehension. Often, this apprehension is strong enough to paralyze you into such a state that you can never gain enough courage to speak out in a group, much less make a formal presentation. Exhibit 2-5 provides some tips for overcoming apprehension about making presentations.

In addition, consider joining groups like Toastmasters to help you overcome any anxiety you have about speaking in front of groups. Other speaking opportunities include schools, civic, and nonprofit organizations. The local chamber of commerce usually maintains a list of organizations anxious to host speakers.

Developing Writing Skills

Close in importance to speaking skills for project managers are writing skills. In project management, there are typically a plethora of reports to complete in addition to the constant requirements for oral communications. It should be obvious that developing these skills to the maximum extent will ensure the greatest success for a project manager.

There has been a steady decline in writing skills during the past forty years. With the advent of television and other electronic media, reading and writing have become less important. With the news available in vivid, graphical detail, there is little reason to bother reading a newspaper or news magazines. Similarly, with the availability of the telephone, e-mail, and teleconferencing, good writing has become far less appealing or used as a means of communication. Although e-mail is technically writing, it is typically used as a fast query-and-response system, with little regard for grammar or sentence structure. In short, the electronic media has sabotaged good writing skills, and people are becoming less comfortable with the written word.

Ironically, even though almost everyone celebrates the infor-

Exhibit 2-5. Tips for overcoming apprehension about speaking.

What to Do	How to Do It
Start small.	Find opportunities in small-group settings, such as church and civic or professional clubs.
Progress slowly; pick slightly larger groups as you gain experience.	Consider Toastmasters or other speaking clubs.
	Consider attending regional meetings of your church or club.
Pick a topic of importance to you.	It is much easier to talk about something you feel strongly about and know something about.
Prepare thoroughly.	Thoroughly research and practice every speech.
	Practice in front of a mirror; practice before a friend, colleague, or family member.
How to do it.	Practice *does* make perfect. Speaking as often as possible makes it easier each time to get before a group.
Scope out the environment.	Always go early to the place for the speech. Knowing the room and its arrangement makes the process more comfortable. Be sure audiovisual equipment is in place and working.
Talk to the friendly faces.	During the speech, find those faces that seem supportive and talk to *them.* Try to locate three or four around the room so that you seem to be encompassing the whole audience as you focus on the friendly ones.
Concentrate completely on the message.	Avoid the pitfall of worrying about what the audience is thinking about you, how you look, or your clothes. Focus only on the subject and getting your points across.

mation technology explosion, most businesspeople I meet are unhappy with their own writing skills, the writing skills of their
employees, or both. No matter how much information technology
takes over the workplace, the power of the written word cannot
be replaced. Given the amount and variety of written reports required of project managers, and the surge by many corporations to
adopt a project management concept of doing business, clearly the
ability to write well is in great demand by employers. Finally, as
Deborah Dumaine, founder of Better Communications, a Boston-
based firm specializing in business, technical, audit, and sales writing workshops, points out, "Skill in writing correlates highly with
the ability to think well—to analyze information, weigh alternatives, and make decisions."[2] This statement epitomizes what is required of good project managera.

Benefits of Writing

Aside from the general benefits of writing already noted, there are
several others as well. One of the greatest is its aid in decision
making. All of us talk to friends or family about decisions we are
wrestling with, and we usually find that talking out the problem
helps us to crystallize our thinking so that we can make a decision
or plan of action. Writing can perform the same function. Many
people find that putting their thoughts on paper helps to clarify the
project or problem they are mulling over.

Just as writing can benefit the writer, it can also benefit the
reader. Some information is too complex or lengthy to explain
orally, particularly over the telephone. Hence, a well-written document provides the reader with complex information in a logical
and clear way that no other medium can.

Steps to Powerful Writing

Writing skills can be learned and developed just as speaking skills
can. Although some people seem to have a gift—their words flow
effortlessly—most of us have to work at writing. It is helpful to
approach writing as a process. With a few steps to guide the process along, writing can become less tedious and much more productive.

One of the major challenges in writing is to be reader-focused—that is, focusing on the reader's needs rather than presenting one's own agenda. Therefore, the following guidelines are developed not only to help make the writing task flow more easily but also to ensure that the writing is reader-focused.

The following steps provide a process for preparing typical project management documents. These steps are the result of many years of experience preparing such documents, and they can be applied in any organization in any industry.

Step 1: What is the purpose of the document, and who gets the information?

In the world of project management, many reports follow a predetermined format. Often, templates of the report are prepared ahead of time, so filling in the blanks is all that is required. Although this approach ensures that reporting is standardized and saves preparation time, it can also create an attitude that the reports are routine. Project management reports may be routine in the sense of reoccurring on a regular basis, but they should never be considered routine information.

This step requires analyzing the purpose of the document and its audience as a result of answering the following questions:

- Why is this document important?
- Who are the readers of this document, and what is their stake in the project?
- What should this report convey to the reader?
- What is the breadth of the reader's understanding of this project now? Would an overview be helpful or required?
- How do I want the readers to react? What type of information or style of presentation of the information will help the readers?
- Of all the information that has to be presented, what is the one thing that I want readers to remember?

Step 2: How much detail is required in the document?

Too many people start writing without giving much thought to the content requirements. It seems to be our nature to want to start on a project immediately, whether the project is writing a report or managing the installation of a complex information technology system, without first going through the planning stage. Nevertheless, all the time spent in planning the writing is more than made up for in the effectiveness, efficiency, and relative ease of completing a comprehensive but concise report. One of the best ways to determine what needs to be in the document is to make an outline. It is simple, straightforward, and applicable to all kinds of documents. In the case of the typical, routinely required project management reports, there will be a corporate policy about format and probably a template to follow. In such cases, using the outline method for generating ideas is applicable, with the template headings serving as major outline headings. Exhibit 2-6 is a typical report template, and Exhibit 2-7 provides a sample of how to incorporate the template into an outline form.

Step 3: Who gets what information?

The communication plan for the project details who needs to be informed of the project's progress. The plan also details the type of information that each recipient needs. For example, the project's sponsor or other senior managers may need detailed information about the project, but other stakeholders only need or want an overview of what is happening. In fact, the financial officer may only want to know what the spending curve looks like against actual expenditures. So the project manager needs to generate ideas and information and sort that information according to the data to be provided.

Once ideas and information have been generated, organize them under appropriate headings. This step should be done without regard to the headings of the standardized report template because using the report headings may be restrictive. That is, there may be information that the target reader needs to be aware of, but it wouldn't quite fit the template. Once the information is organized under appropriate headings (or categories), you can transfer the data into the correct template headings. The objective in this step is to ensure that all pertinent data is included in the final report.

Exhibit 2-6. Typical report format.

STATUS REPORT

Project: Report Date:

Phase: Report Period:

Project Manager:

Summary of Progress:

Project Issues/Problems/Action Taken:

Planned Activities for Next Reporting Period:

Potential Problems/Issues During Next Period:

Recommendations:

Request of Action/Decisions:

Exhibit 2-7. Traditional outline for generating ideas for project reports.

I. Overview of Project Progress
   A. Summary of work planned
   B. Summary of work accomplished
   C. Attachments of budget reports
   D. Attachments of schedules
   E. Budget and schedule variances

II. Summary of Issues/Problems Encountered During This Period
   A. Statement of each issue/problem with action taken
   B. Summary of impact of each issue/problem on overall project budget or schedule

III. Planned Activities for Next Reporting Period
   A. Key activities with person/group responsible
   B. Special milestones
   C. List and description of meetings planned
   D. Deliverables due

IV. Recommendations and Requests for Action
   A. Description of recommended approval or action needed (if any)
   B. Approval chain
   C. Required action from each level

Step 4: What is the frequency of the document, and how can it be most effective?

This may be the key step in the process of writing the report because it is the one that helps you concentrate the focus of the report on the one or two most important points. A way to focus the information is to sequence it according to who needs it and what the impact of the information will be. Sequencing the information means to examine all the information that has been generated to determine the key points and then to place these points in the most obvious part of the report for the appropriate recipient.

Most people tend to write much as they think. That is, they think in a linear fashion, from the first step in the process they want to describe to the last. If they write in the same way, the most important piece of information will be in the last sentence. Most of the time, the last sentence should become the first sentence in order to highlight the important point. Therefore, once you have organized the information, examine it with the view of moving the most important statements to the beginning of each heading.

Step 5. Is there a template for the document?

Many organizations, usually through their project management office, provide templates for project reports. This practice provides a ready-made format that can be used to prepare the report. Unfortunately, these templates do not cover every stockholder's need— that is, those who need more or less information. So the project manager may have to revise the template, but regardless of whether the template fits the situation exactly, the template should be used as the basis for developing the document.

Step 6: How important is the first draft?

Using the information that now has been organized and properly sequenced, write the first draft, using the report template if one is required. Do not fall into the trap of trying to edit the document as you write this draft; this will only restrict the flow of ideas and hamper your efforts to include all pertinent information. Address each heading of the report as quickly as possible without regard to the amount of information being supplied. The objective here is to get as much mileage from the document as possible—that is, to use the document to describe completely and thoroughly the problem, status, or whatever message you need to transmit. More is better in this case, at least to the extent that free rein is given to your effort to be thorough in presenting all relevant project information.

Step 7: How do I edit the document?

Editing a report is considerably easier than generating it. That is why it is important to resist the editing process until last. Cutting out superfluous information, words, or phrases—and, therefore, making the document more concise—is easier to do from the complete document than if there is still a need to add more information. Having to add information as an afterthought can make the writing sound disjointed and disorganized. Follow the editing checklist in Exhibit 2-8 to ensure that your editing is thorough. In the final step of the editing process—editing for style, punctuation, and grammar—the best reference is still Strunk and White's *The Elements of Style*.[3]

Becoming an Active Listener

Listening is important. The average worker spends about 50 percent of his or her business hours listening, but research has shown that the average person only listens with 25 percent efficiency. That means that if 100 million workers each made one $10 listening mistake per year, the cost to business is $1 billion.

The authors of one research study concluded that listening is related to other communication abilities and to success at work.

Exhibit 2-8. Self-editing checklist.

Purpose of Report	Stated clearly?
	Specific statement about needed action?
Information	Complete and accurate?
Sequence of Information	Most important statements at top of report?
	Ideas and information flowing logically?
Attachments	Pictures or graphics attached to clarify information?
Paragraph/Section Structure	Sentences and paragraphs concise and brief?
Words	Free of acronyms or defined?
	Free of clichés and jargon?
	Active verbs used?
Proofread	Spelling checked?
	Grammar correct?
	Punctuation correct?

Better listeners, they found, hold higher positions and are promoted more often than those who have less developed listening skills.[4]

Barriers to Listening

The following story is told about Franklin Delano Roosevelt and his belief that most people are poor listeners:

> Franklin Delano Roosevelt, thirty-second president of the United States, found the polite small talk of social functions at the White House somewhat tedious. He maintained that those present on such occasions rarely paid much attention to what was said to them. To illustrate the point, he would sometimes amuse himself by greeting guests with the words, "I murdered my grandmother this morning." The response was invariably one of polite approval. On one occasion, however, the president happened upon an attentive listener. On hearing Roosevelt's outrageous remark, the guest replied diplomatically, "I'm sure she had it coming to her."[5]

President Roosevelt was right, though: Most people do not pay close attention to what is being said. There are several barriers to listening to blame, such as:

- Inability to hear because the speaker doesn't speak loudly enough or doesn't enunciate clearly
- Hearing impairment
- Paying more attention to the speaker's characteristics—clothes, words, voice, accent, and so on—than to the speaker's meaning
- Preconceived beliefs or opinions about the subject that preclude hearing the speaker's ideas
- Thinking of what to say at the next pause in the conversation
- Fatigue
- Noise
- Visual distractions such as people coming into the room or into the field of vision

- Trying to think of two things at once
- Inability to focus on what the speaker is saying

One of the major problems of listening is that our thought processes move much faster than the spoken word. The average speaker speaks at a rate of about 130 words a minute, but our thought processes operate several times faster. Consequently, active listening requires concentrated attention on the speaker.

I was present at a victory party for Senator John Warner of Virginia while he was married to the actress Elizabeth Taylor. Naturally, Elizabeth Taylor received a great deal of attention at the party, and I enjoyed watching her make her way through the crowd of people as they eagerly vied for a chance to talk with her. The one thing that most struck me was the way she gave her undivided attention to each person who spoke to her. By her concentrated focus on each of the speakers, she made it clear that whatever they had to say was very important, and she was anxious to hear it. Being an effective listener requires this kind of concentration and focus.

Gaining Perspectives on Listening

There are two perspectives of listening that are found in the project manager's world: facilitative and critical listening.[6]

Keys to Facilitative Listening

Facilitative listening means listening well, being courteous and constructive, and reacting to the speaker in an appropriate way. There are several key strategies to becoming a facilitative listener (which are also summarized in Exhibit 2-9):

Be prepared. Being a prepared listener is every bit as important as being a prepared speaker. However, being prepared to listen isn't always possible. That is, if the opportunity to listen is the result of an unexpected one-on-one encounter, there may be no way to anticipate the topic of conversation. But if the meeting was requested, know what the meeting is about and be prepared to respond appropriately. What I mean by being pre-

Exhibit 2-9. Strategies for becoming a facilitative listener.

Listening Strategies	Preparation Strategies
Be prepared.	Read all materials prior to any meetings.
Listen to fit the purpose.	Listen with the appropriated seriousness and concentration that the meeting deserves. Project progress meetings require greater attention than team social gatherings.
Allocate adequate time for the meeting.	Scope the meeting, and resist telephone or other interruptions.
Look past the speaker's external characteristics.	Don't let the speaker's clothes, voice tone, or message put you off. Focus on the speaker's purpose.
Listen to the speaker.	Force yourself to maintain eye contact. Don't be disturbed by other activities in the area.
Be a responsive listener.	Respond to the speaker by nodding or with other nonverbal signals to let her know that you are listening and understand.
Ask for clarification.	Ask questions to show the speaker you are interested and to make sure you understand completely what is being said.
Think before asking questions, be brief, and be concise.	Never dominate the discussion. Always try to make comments or ask questions that are relevant and insightful. Be brief.

(continues)

Exhibit 2-9. (Continued.)

Listening Strategies	Preparation Strategies
Help the speaker toward mutual understanding.	Sometimes a speaker can lose track of what is causing a misunderstanding in the discussion. Be helpful by rephrasing the questions or adding comments that clarify the problem.
Listen with perspective.	Overlook speaker or presentation flaws. Focus on the important points of the message.

pared applies more to opportunities involving prearranged meetings. A facilitative listener will have read the agenda and any other background material available before arriving at the meeting.

Listen to fit the purpose. The purpose of the meeting will signal what type of listening is needed. If an individual team member requests a meeting to discuss a personal issue, the facilitative listener will be prepared to be empathetic and listen with the appropriate level of concern and support. If the meeting is a team meeting to discuss the status of a project task, then a high level of critical and interactive listening is required. If the meeting is for entertaining or for recognizing a team member's work, listening noncritically is called for. Facilitative listeners adapt to the appropriate level of listening to fit the purpose of the meeting.

Allocate adequate time for the meeting. There are few things more annoying than having members of a team move in and out of a meeting or for a person to interrupt a meeting to take telephone calls. In a busy environment, it is not possible to avoid all the interruptions; nevertheless, the facilitative listener and smart listener will allot enough time to complete the meeting with minimum interruptions. The benefit is to both the speaker and the listener.

Look past the speaker's external characteristics. We often tune out a speaker because we don't like the person's looks, manner of speaking, accent, or message. The facilitative listener will look beyond all that to the speaker's purpose. The message may be needed information, pleasant or not, and by not giving the speaker a fair hearing, the message will be missed.

Listen to the speaker. Whatever else is going on around the conversation or in the listener's life, the facilitative listener will put it out of his or her mind and concentrate completely on the speaker. Concentrating in such a focused way isn't easy to do and requires effort. The next time you are talking with someone, take note of how hard it is to maintain eye contact and not look away to see who just came into the room or what made the noise outside. In a meeting, the eye contact should still be there, and listening to the speaker means not carrying on side conversations or reading the report you brought along.

Be a responsive listener. A good listener will always respond in some way to the speaker—a nod to show agreement or some other nonverbal body movement to indicate attentive listening. Mrs. Johnson, my high school math teacher, after explaining some involved mathematical manipulation, once grabbed my sleeve and shook it vigorously. When she was sure she had my attention, she asked if I understood the mathematical derivation she had just explained. Upon answering in the affirmative, she said, "Well, change your face!" What Mrs. Johnson was saying to me is that I wasn't being a responsive listener; I wasn't "changing my face" to indicate comprehension or even that I was listening.

Ask for clarification. One of the best methods of keeping yourself focused on the conversation, showing the speaker that you are interested in what is being said, and making certain that you understand what was said, is to ask for clarification periodically. In a one-on-one situation, this is not hard to do, but in a group, people are reluctant to ask questions for fear of appearing stupid. The fact is, if one person isn't clear on a point, then there usually are others who didn't understand it either. From the speaker's perspective, it is better to have a chance to clarify points early than to continue talking about something that is baffling to the audience.

Think before asking questions, be brief, and be concise. Whether in a group or in a one-on-one situation, the facilitative listener will wait for a convenient breaking point to ask questions or make comments and then will be as brief and to the point as possible.

Help the speaker toward mutual understanding. In group meetings, it is not unusual for a speaker to become confused or unable to see the solution to a snag in the conversation. A facilitative listener will help resolve this difficulty or problem by offering examples or by rephrasing the issue. In a one-on-one situation, there will be times when one individual has some difficulty expressing himself, particularly if the problem is a personal one and talking about it is difficult. The facilitative listener's role is to make the speaker feel safe by establishing rapport and creating a climate of trust.

Listen with perspective. The facilitative listener will overlook any flaws or minor problems with a speaker or presentation to focus on the major points of what is being said. The good listener can separate the wheat from the chaff and will focus only on the important points of the message.

Keys to Critical Listening

Critical listening is on a different level of listening than facilitative listening, but they are not mutually exclusive. Facilitative listening can be thought of as listening in a way that helps the speaker present his or her message. *Critical listening* is listening to spot the flaws and to cut through the rhetoric to the heart of the issues. There are several key strategies to becoming a critical listener (as summarized in Exhibit 2-10):

Look beyond technique to substance. Everyone is familiar with the type of speaker who is so polished that no one can remember exactly what his message was but liked him anyway because he was so dynamic or spoke so beautifully. Politicians have the reputation of being able to speak in broad terms and clichés so

Exhibit 2-10. Strategies for becoming a critical listener.

Look beyond technique to substance.	Look beyond the glitz and showmanship and discard all that does not add value.
Look for the importance of the ideas.	Always ask yourself what the point of the message is.
Insist on specifics, not generalities.	Require the speaker to focus on details, not make general or vague statements.
Question the assumptions.	The end results are directly related to the beginning assumptions. Be sure to examine and question the assumptions to ensure that the logic being followed is valid.
Demand evidence.	Ask the speaker to cite evidence for statements made as fact.

that they are not pinned down to specifics. Critical listening cuts through this type of presentation and discards anything that was said that did not add value or substance.

Look for the importance of the ideas. Ask the question, "What is the point of all this?" If there is no point, then the information should be discarded. It is more often the case than not that the speaker is trying to make certain key points but sometimes has difficulty getting directly to the point. Question the speaker to determine where the presentation is going if that appears to be the case. Keep the speaker on track and focused on providing information that will clarify the points being made.

Insist on specifics, not generalities. Whether one-on-one or in a group, the critical listener insists that the speaker focus on details and not hide behind general statements. The statement by a task leader, "We will make up the schedule slippage by the end of the month," sounds good, but asking how it is going to be done might reveal that there is no workable plan in place to do it. In the world of project management, there is no substitute for one of Colin Powell's laws: "Pay attention to the small things."[7]

Question the assumptions. The end results are directly related to the beginning assumptions. In project management, assumptions are made all the time. The critical listener will always test the assumptions to ensure that the logic being followed is valid. Whenever a team member presents a solution to a project problem, be sure that the assumptions are clear and valid, given the best information available.

Demand evidence. The critical listener will always question the assumptions and ask that the speaker cite evidence for statements made as facts. Too many people present data or information based on unverified facts. The project manager's job is to make sure that each team member operates from the perspective that all facts are verified and any information provided by the team can be substantiated.

Summary

Communication is the basis of all human endeavor. How well we succeed in life is directly related to our ability to communicate, and this is particularly true in the world of project management.

Given the process of communication with its inherent problems of filtering by the messenger and the receiver, the noise that invariably intrudes into the process, and our own lack of understanding about the art of communication, it is not surprising that messages go astray. To mitigate these problems, we can strive to improve our verbal communication skills, particularly speaking, writing, and listening.

CHAPTER 3

Negotiation Skills

Let every eye negotiate for itself and trust no agent.

—WILLIAM SHAKESPEARE
Much Ado About Nothing

The skill employed most by project managers but discussed the least is the negotiation skill. Considering that the work life of a project manager is filled with conflict, it is surprising that so few project management texts present negotiation skills and strategies in any real depth. Yet project managers have to deal with numerous sources of conflict, and in a manner that does not alienate anyone. Developing this skill should be a high priority for project managers; if they aren't good negotiators, they should start looking for a new job.

This chapter addresses the primary causes of conflict in a project and the skills and personal qualities required to cope with the conflict. The chapter closes with a set of guidelines for preparing and executing a negotiation event.[1]

Sources of Conflict in a Project

Conflict often arises during a project's life cycle because of one of the following:[2]

- *Priorities*—that is, which projects have priority, and do the projects' priority overshadow general functional work?
- *Policies and procedures*—that is, the lack of consistency of project procedures (and tools) available to the project team.
- *Technical trade-offs*—often a problem resulting from a lack of expertise within the organization or because of disagreements among various functional groups about the best technical approach.
- *Staffing*—organizations attempt to hire staff for specific contracts. Hence, new contracts often do not have the requisite staff available when a project starts.
- *Cost estimates*—organizations usually underestimate project costs, either because of inadequate estimating techniques or because of the need to offer a low bid to win a contract.
- *Schedules*—usually underestimated because the team and project manager are optimistic that nothing will go wrong and the project will be finished without problems occurring.
- *Psychology*—there are two sources of conflict in this category; general personality conflict and conflict because one or more of the team members are reluctant to complete their work because they do not want the project to end.

One or more of these areas will be the focus of the conflict, but the conflict itself typically is the result of a difference of opinion. Five groups of people have an interest in one or more of these areas of conflict:

- The customer
- Functional and senior managers
- Project team members
- Other stakeholders
- Vendors

Negotiating with vendors is usually the responsibility of a procurement or contracting staff member, not the project manager, so I will not address this area.[3]

All seven sources of conflict are present throughout the project, but the intensity of each varies with the phase of the project. In Part II, we examine each area of conflict, and I explain why they become more intense in one project phase than in another. This chapter will concentrate on identifying the parties at interest for each of the conflict sources and show how the project manager can deal with them.

The Customer

The project manager is the key contact person for the client or customer. The depth and complexity of negotiations with the customer vary according to whether the customer is external or internal to the project organization. If the customer is external to the organization, the project manager often is responsible for the proposal leading to a contract award and sometimes participates in the contract negotiations. This kind of negotiation is far more complex and adversarial than those that deal with an internal customer. With an internal customer, the project manager is negotiating with friends and allies (this is presuming there is a congenial and collegial corporate environment). However, these two scenarios require the same skills and the same negotiation guidelines.

The customer is interested in schedules, budgets, and product specifications. Hence, these will be the primary causes of any conflict between the project manager and the customer.

Functional and Senior Management

The functional manager has control of the personnel resources that the project manager needs to staff the project. The project manager must negotiate with the functional managers for these resources and often must often battle to keep the resources assigned to the project when functional priorities change. The functional managers also have strong opinions about the technical approach of a project. The project manager similarly negotiates regularly with senior management regarding project priority and their commitment.

Project Team Members

In working with the project team, the project manager acts more like a mediator than a negotiator. A team member might negotiate with the project manager to do one task that is more interesting or challenging than the one assigned. For the most part, however, the relationship between the project manager and the team member is more of a leader and a follower. The real problem for the project manager in a team setting is to mediate between the team members and to resolve any personality conflicts that occur.

Other Stakeholders

Other stakeholders include people who do not have a direct involvement in the project but do have an interest in it because it could have an impact on their function. For instance, someone from finance would not have a direct interest in the technical aspects of the project but does have an interest in how it affects cash flow or profits. A functional manager might not have any involvement in the project now but might have the responsibility for maintaining the end product. Dealing with these stakeholders requires the project manager to be part negotiator and part politician.

The wise project manager will determine all the stakeholders early in the project cycle and relate their goals to the project's goals. Most people avoid using the word *politics* when speaking of their job. However, polishing and exercising one's political skill is crucial to success, especially in dealing with stakeholders. The project manager's influence is fragile at best, and exercising his or her political skill is one way to build influence.

In his book on project politics, J. Davidson Frame defines a three-step process that a good project politician follows:[4]

1. *Assess the Environment.* In assessing the environment, the project manager must be sensitive to the corporate goals and strategies and who the relevant stakeholders are. The environment of the company is determined by the corporate culture and by the

company's current competitive status. If the culture is not a collegial and supportive one, the project manager needs to exercise considerable political skill. Even if the culture is collegial and supportive, it is not unusual to discover at least one person who is against the project. When this situation occurs, it is crucial for the project manager to identify the person and try to assuage his or her concerns. An unhappy stakeholder can undermine a project before the unwary project manager knows what is happening.

2. *Identify the goals of the principal actors.* Once the stakeholders are identified, the project manager must ascertain their goals. What drives these people? Do they have a hidden agenda? If so, how can the project manager deal with this hidden agenda? It is not easy to determine what drives some people. That is probably why many project managers, even professional project managers, do not bother with these steps. They jump straight into problem solving and finding solutions. What they fail to understand until it is too late is that stakeholders can make or break a project. Making sure the project goals are consistent with those of the stakeholder is the surest way to obtain and keep them as allies.

3. *Assess your own capabilities.* Successful project managers know their own strengths and weaknesses and how best to capitalize on their strengths. Once the project manager identifies the stakeholders and their goals, he or she needs to mitigate any negative feelings or reservations about supporting the project. Without an objective self-analysis and a critical evaluation of one's capabilities, the project manager will find that dealing successfully with people's problems, particularly those external to the project, becomes impossible.

Once these three steps—assessing the environment, identifying the goals, and assessing one's own capability—are accomplished, the project manager is able to define the problem in order to develop and refine proper solutions. It bears repeating that the nature of the project manager's influence is fragile under the best of conditions, and political savvy is one way to enhance or increase one's influence in the company.

The Skills and Personal Qualities of a Good Negotiator

Successful negotiators have three key skills—communication, listening, and judgment—and three personal qualities—honesty, flexibility, and credibility.

Honesty

Honesty is the single most important personal quality of a successful project manager. Almost every other mistake a person makes can be overcome and forgiven, but not dishonesty. Once a person lies, no one fully trusts the person again, and his or her influence and effectiveness are ruined. Nevertheless, many professional project managers will risk damaging their credibility and will violate their integrity rather than admit that they are having a problem with a project. This is a serious failing.

Sometimes the project manager is caught in the difficult situation of being directed by a senior manager not to reveal a problem to the customer. The rationale is that the problem will be corrected without the customer ever being the wiser. In this situation, you have to evaluate your ethical code and decide whether your conscience will allow the lie and if you are willing to risk your professional reputation.

Certainly some judgment is required about the seriousness of a problem. Every project has problems, but the problems we are discussing here are those that transcend the daily snags, irritations, and false starts. The customer will not be interested in these problems. However, if the problem is severe enough to cause a delay or requires a short-term infusion of additional resources, the customer needs to know about it. The customer will *not* be upset that the project manager encountered a problem; however, the customer *will* be upset to learn of the problem after it is so big that there is a significant impact on the project. The customer knows there are going to be problems in every project. Do not insult the customer's intelligence by pretending no problems exist in your project; he or she will not believe it. Remember that customers will accept problems as long as they can be a part of the solution.

Flexibility

The project manager usually works in a matrix organization, which means that the project team members come from functional groups throughout the company. It also means that the project manager does not have direct control over the company's personnel and must negotiate with the various functional managers for their use. Consequently, she or he must know what skill level is needed for the project, and there must be an alternative choice if the ideal candidate is not available to work on the project. In today's environment, the functional manager is usually willing to assign the requested person to a specific project, but that person may already be working on one or more projects. Hence, to have access to a particular person may require juggling schedules, taking the desired person for odd or random periods, and supplementing the desired person with other people. Sometimes a particular person may be available only for some supervisory duties or as a consultant to the project. All this requires the project manager to be very knowledgeable about the goals and objectives, schedule, and required product quality and to be flexible in her or his approach to resource negotiations.

Credibility

Credibility means that the project manager is known to be knowledgeable, capable, dependable, and a person of integrity. A reputation for credibility is earned; it cannot be established overnight, and it will not be believed until it is demonstrated. This quality is something that the project manager must work at with patience and persistence. The only way to be credible is to deliver as promised, be honest in all dealings, and be consistent in behavior.

If these words sound remarkably like those in the discussion about honesty, it should not be surprising. The two are not mutually exclusive. You cannot have one without the other.

Communication Skills

The project manager is the spokesperson for the project. I remember as an engineering student having to take a course that required researching a topic and formally presenting the results to the class; essentially this was a public speaking course, but oriented to engineers presenting technical information. One of my classmates complained often and loudly about having to take the course. "I'm going to be an engineer, not a public speaker," he protested. "I don't need a public-speaking course." How wrong he was! People who cannot communicate well are severely limited. In addition, people who are more proficient at communication are more successful.

Listening Skills

Being a good listener is key to being a good communicator. Many people seem to define communication as the art of speaking effectively but forget that good communication requires dialogue. They forget the other half of the communication equation: listening. Usually we are so busy thinking of what we are going to say next that we don't listen to what the other person is saying. Worse, periods of silence make us uneasy so we feel compelled to continue talking past anything meaningful. It is impossible to listen when you are talking.

Good Judgment

A colleague once told me that judgment is innate; either you have it or you don't. I disagree. Judgment is a skill that can be developed. Good judgment is based on knowledge of the subject, the ability to project what the consequences of the judgment will be, the ability for problem solving and generating alternative solutions, and the capacity for making decisions. Exercising patience and drawing on all the other skills of a project manager will enhance the project manager's judgment, and a system for making good decisions can be developed. The following four steps can lead to good judgment decisions:

1. Study the problem or planned course of action.
2. List the potential risks and consequences of the decision.

3. Generate alternative solutions or modify the original solution.

4. Make the decision.

Good judgment not only means providing solutions, courses of action, or solving problems. It means knowing when and how to say no to unreasonable constraints placed by senior management or the customer. It means knowing when to tell the customer that certain new changes cannot be accommodated within the current scope of the contract. It means knowing when to go to senior management for help rather than admitting a problem is beyond your current capability or control.

Negotiating Guidelines

Roger Fisher and William Ury's excellent book, *Getting to Yes,* is a superb negotiation primer that presents what the authors call "principled negotiation."[5] Principled negotiation assumes a win-win solution and thus must be the project manager's approach. When the project manager negotiates, he or she is negotiating with friends and allies, not adversaries, and the negotiations are for the long-term benefit of the company, not for any individual. There are four steps in principled negotiation:

1. Separate the people from the problem.
2. Focus on interests, not positions.
3. Create options.
4. Insist on standards.

I have expanded the concept to seven steps, which can serve as a checklist for negotiation preparations and execution. The principled negotiation steps are incorporated in the guidelines shown in Exhibit 3-1.

Step 1: Prepare

The project manager should be the most knowledgeable person about the project. Many projects are the result of a competitive bid

Exhibit 3-1. Guidelines for successful negotiations.

Guidelines	Strategies
Step 1: Prepare.	Know everything possible about the project.
	Profile the person with whom you are negotiating.
Step 2: Be sensitive to different perceptions.	Separate people from the problem.
	Understand that each person's view of the project may be different.
	Focus on interests, not positions.
Step 3: Use creativity and imagination.	Create options.
	Be flexible.
Step 4: Help others to agree with your proposal.	Use standards, published procedures, and corporate goals.
Step 5: Value any deadlines you agree to.	Never violate the agreements made with functional managers and team members.
Step 6: Take notes and follow up with a record outlining the agreements.	Always provide a written record of the agreements each party made.
Step 7: Prepare for no agreement, but leave with an intact relationship.	Be prepared in case no agreement is possible.
	Leave every negotiation with the relationship intact.

in which a proposal was submitted in response to a formal, written solicitation called a request for proposal or invitation for bid. In those cases, there will be project specifications, a statement of work, a contract document, and a proposal that provides a complete project management plan. The project manager is responsible for having a thorough knowledge of each of these documents and should be prepared to explain any or all of them when she enters into negotiations with senior and functional managers, other stakeholders, and the customer.

A project that is assigned within the organization and not having written specifications or a project plan requires special consideration by the project manager. The project manager is responsible for writing a plan (the format and purpose of a project management plan is discussed in Part Two of this book) and collecting all possible data about the project's goals, scope, objectives, and budget.

Complete technical knowledge about the project is only half the preparation equation. The project manager should also identify the stakeholders and other functional managers she has to negotiate with and prepare a profile of each one of them before negotiations begin. Knowing all you can about the other person—their goals and how they view your project—before you meet with them is crucial for a successful negotiation.

Step 2: Be Sensitive to Different Perceptions

Every person will have a slightly different, and sometimes radically different, perspective of the project. Even after everyone agrees about the goals of the project, the approaches to reaching these goals will differ. The wise project manager will be sensitive to these different viewpoints and be open to them. Determining the interests of each person isn't always easy, but focusing on their interests and not on their stated positions leads to a faster agreement and usually enriches the solutions.

One of the most serious mistakes a negotiator can make is to attack his or her opponent—or in our case the functional or senior manager, customer, or other stakeholder—rather than the problem. Attacking the person only makes him or her defensive and resistant to any proposal. Concentrating on the problem and soliciting the person's assistance most often results in solving the problem for mutual gain. Remember that these people have their own agenda; although they may be interested in helping with your project, it probably is not their first priority. They have other responsibilities that take precedence, and they usually are already supporting several other company projects.

Step 3: Use Creativity and Imagination

Flexibility is the key to negotiating with functional managers for scarce resources. The project manager has a requirement for particular skills and will have certain people in mind for the tasks. However, the desired people may not be available at the optimum time, or at all, during the period of the project. In that case, you must be ready with other options. For instance, perhaps the person you really want is available to provide guidance and support to a less experienced person.

Step 4: Help Others to Agree with Your Position

A great general once said that you should always build a bridge so that your enemies would have a way to flee. You shouldn't view those with whom you negotiate as enemies, but building a bridge so that they have a way of retreating is smart. Helping those with whom you negotiate to agree with your position is building a bridge for them. The bridge allows them to modify their position and to accept your recommendations.

Citing corporate goals and objectives and relating them to the project goals and objectives will make it much easier for a functional manager to accede to your requests for help. When functional managers can visualize clearly how their involvement with the project furthers their goals and those of the company, they will work harder to support the project.

Step 5: Value Any Deadlines You Agree To

Winning the battle but losing the war is an old cliché but one that perfectly describes the consequences of not adhering to agreed deadlines. Remember that most of the time, functional managers have made adjustments in their operating schedules to accommodate your requests for resources. When you agree to release a person at a specific time, the functional manager is presuming that that person will be available for other projects then. If you ignore the agreed-to deadline, the functional manager may have no choice but to withdraw support.

If you have agreed to certain deadlines but cannot meet them because of a change in the project, then continued use of the person or equipment must be renegotiated. This situation may create a new set of problems that have to be resolved. Addressing the issue with the responsible manager most likely will create an ally rather than an adversary.

Step 6: Take Notes and Follow Up with a Record Outlining Agreements

Most professional project managers I know fail to take notes during their negotiations and seldom follow up the discussions with a record of agreements. Usually this is because doing so is just one more thing they have to do in an already too busy schedule. Yet consider how often we think we have an agreement, only to discover later that one party interpreted the agreement differently from another. Also, it is worthwhile to have a record of agreements to ensure that you know when the functional managers are expecting to have their people available for other projects. Finally, having the results of all your negotiations on record relieves you of the burden of having to remember everything. Your life is too busy to rely on memory, no matter how good it is.

Step 7: Prepare for No Agreement but Leave the Negotiation with an Intact Relationship

Perhaps the most damaging thing that can happen during a negotiation is to destroy the relationship between the two participants. The reality of everyday business is that no company or functional manager has enough resources to accommodate every project manager's request. Consequently, there will be times when you walk away without an agreement to support the project. Unfortunately, too many project managers believe that their project is the most important business initiative in the company, and they take a rebuff as a personal affront. They often become angry and attack the person they view as being uncooperative. Even if this project manager successfully reverses the original decision, imagine how successful he or she will be in the future.

Remember Step 2, and separate the person from the problem.

If you are unsuccessful in obtaining the support you need from a
functional manager, remember that there will be another time
when you need the person's help. Parting on good terms can only
help when next you approach this person for help.

Summary

The work of a project manager is a life of conflict. Although conflict is not necessarily bad, it is an issue that has to be resolved by
the project manager. Without excellent negotiations skills, a project manager has little chance for success.

Conflict in a project's life cycle can be attributed to one or more
of the following areas:

- Project priorities
- Administrative procedures
- Technical trade-offs
- Staffing
- Support cost estimates
- Schedules
- Personalities

To deal with the conflict areas of a project, the following seven
steps have been developed:

- *Step 1:* Prepare.
- *Step 2:* Be sensitive to different perceptions, and separate the
  people from the problem.
- *Step 3:* Use creativity and imagination.
- *Step 4:* Help others to agree with your position.
- *Step 5:* Value any deadlines you agree to.
- *Step 6:* Take notes and follow up with a record outlining
  agreements.

- *Step 7:* Prepare for no agreement but leave the negotiation with an intact relationship.

Following these guidelines will help you approach each conflict issue or situation with greater confidence, and they will ensure a greater chance for success.

CHAPTER 4

Leadership Skills

Leadership and learning are indispensable to each other.

—JOHN F. KENNEDY
(1917–1963)
from a speech prepared for delivery in Dallas, November 22, 1963

The traditional view of management and leadership is that management is concerned with efficiently and effectively using a company's resources to accomplish the company's business, while leadership is more concerned with innovation, challenging the status quo, and broadening the company's outlook and capabilities. Managers try to get people to work more efficiently; leaders try to get people to agree about the things that need to be done.[1]

Project managers have three basic responsibilities in managing a project; to be on or under budget, to be on or ahead of schedule, and to meet certain performance criteria (the quality requirements as defined by the customer for the end product). This is a restatement of my definition of project management from the first edition of this book. Therefore, project managers certainly must have the management skills needed to accomplish the project's goals successfully. What many people do not recognize is that project managers also must be leaders. Leadership qualities are even more crucial in an environment of organizational downsizing and the trend toward organizations that are flat or have fewer layers of middle and senior management. With downsizing, there is more work to do with fewer people, and there are morale problems resulting from feelings of job insecurity. With flatter organizations, the project manager is in a more visible position, and the project is more subject to senior management involvement.

There is an overlap of management and leadership. Clearly, not every manager is a leader, nor is every leader a manager. However, the more successful project managers I know exhibit a high degree of leadership capability. This is evidenced by the higher level of morale in one project team compared with another, by the fewer problems encountered during the life of one project than occur in another, the ability of one team to finish the project on or under budget and schedule, and the high degree of customer satisfaction found in some projects and not in others. These high-performance teams are sure signs of project manager leadership.

Types of Leadership

It is a simplification to say that types of leadership can be described either as autocratic and authoritarian or democratic and egalitarian. Clearly there are many variations of these two extremes, but I focus on these two only because there are just two ways of changing a follower's behavior: A leader can alter the follower's information or knowledge about a task (which is the *autocratic* approach) or alter the follower's motivation toward the task (which is the *egalitarian* approach). An explanation of these types of leadership will suffice to make clear what the project manager should strive for in the role of leader.

A great many studies have contrasted the authoritarian and democratic concepts of leadership. Exhibit 4-1 provides a summary of the differences between these two concepts.

Authoritarian leaders get jobs done, but they are more concerned about the tasks or products than about the employees. In the long term, this approach of leadership can be devastating to the organization, but it can be of value, depending on what organizations need at that instant. For example, authoritarian leaders can provide structure and information, but only the information they

Exhibit 4-1. Autocratic and democratic leadership skills.

Autocratic (or task-related)	Democratic (or person-related)
Authoritarian	Egalitarian
Product- or task-related	Person-related
Persuasive	Permissive
Goal achievement–oriented	Group maintenance–oriented
Punitive	Nonpunitive
Directive	Joint decision making
Charismatic	Consensual
Closed discussion and decision making	Open discussion and decision making
Nonrewarding	Rewarding

deem pertinent or necessary. They also make decisions about what must be done, make rules, promise rewards, and threaten punishment for failure or disobedience.[2] These leaders depend on their position and knowledge of policy to regulate the behavior of employees.

A democratic or egalitarian leader will actively involve him- or herself in the leadership role, but this leader's emphasis will be on the employee and relationships. This type of leader is more interested in subordinates' contributions to the process or team, encourages consensus decision making, and seeks out subordinates for input before making a decision.

Effects of Authoritarian Leadership

Authoritarian leadership is seen as being dictatorial or managing by intimidation. This style of leadership is the most difficult style to balance so that its use does not create resentment of or resistance to the leader. To achieve balance with this style requires the leader to recognize its appropriate use while being sensitive to the consequences of the style if it is not employed judiciously.

When Authoritarian Leadership Is Better

Certain professions or certain situations require an authoritarian leader. The military is an obvious profession, where the authoritarian leadership style is required because of the nature and rapidity with which decisions have to be made. It has been shown that military officers who established a high level of discipline were more likely to be rated much higher by their superiors.[3] Similarly, it was shown that U.S. Air Force aircrews who received feedback by highly authoritarian methods exhibited greater improvement in performance.

When Authoritarian Leadership Is Worse

When authoritarian leadership includes punitive and disciplinary actions, productivity tends to deteriorate. Punishment increases tension in individuals and groups. Employees who are singled out for punishment exhibit resentment, and they tend to infect the rest of the group with their resentment. The leader suffers from a loss of respect and credibility, and the entire process begins to deteriorate. As morale and performance diminish, the autocratic leader reacts by increasing pressure and threatening more discipline, thus hastening the demise of the project, process, or group. The wall plaque that announces that BEATINGS WIIL CONTINUE UNTIL MORALE IMPROVES is based on a degree of fact—there are leaders who think this way.

Effects of Democratic or Egalitarian Leadership

In almost every circumstance, democratic or egalitarian leadership is the best leadership style. It can be carried to extremes, though, if the leader doesn't balance the democratic leadership style against the team's and the project's needs.

When Democratic Leadership Is Better

Supervisors with democratic leadership styles are characterized by adequate authority, communication downward, sympathy, lack of arbitrariness, and lack of hypercritical attitudes toward employees.

These supervisors are rated by higher management as being more effective than supervisors who exhibit less democratic behavior. Furthermore, their subordinates exhibit higher morale and are more productive.

Generally, it is agreed that in a person-oriented environment, employees or team members are happier and productivity is greater. Democratic leadership is effective in any team environment, provided the leader recognizes that his or her ultimate responsibility is to ensure that the team is functioning smoothly and productively. Fulfilling that responsibility can require the leader to make decisions outside the democratic process. Hence, a democratic leadership style is preferable in project management, but it must be balanced against the urgency of project requirements.

When Democratic Leadership Is Worse

Even good things can be carried to extreme. A leadership style that consistently reinforces the correct performance of team members by approval and suggestions for improvement results in better performance and higher achievement than if they are permitted maximum participation, as in the democratic style. Hence, democratic leadership without sensitivity to the individual's needs for fulfillment and achievement will have an adverse effect on the team. The challenge for the leader, then, is to balance his or her democratic leadership style against the team's and the project's needs.

Leadership Qualities That Followers Expect of a Project Manager

An in-depth study identified a number of characteristics important in a leader.[4] The top four were honest, competent, forward-looking, and inspiring.

Honest

Being honest was the characteristic most often mentioned by those responding to the survey. In my years as a project manager working with Department of Defense (DOD) customers, I also found that each time a customer had a complaint about a contractor's representative, it was most often because of that person's credibility, the basis of which is honesty.

Project managers make a serious mistake when they attempt to hide problems from their superiors or the customer. A project manager who tells the customer that everything is fine in the project when it isn't risks losing the confidence of the customer or, worse, having the contract terminated. In my experience, the customer never minds that the project has problems. Every project has problems! What the customer wants is to be a part of the solution.

Honesty is the cornerstone of credibility. You establish your credibility by your actions. If you are honest in all your dealings, it will be obvious, and your credibility will be established.

Competent

Being competent does not mean that the project manager needs to be an expert in all the skill sets of the project. Rather, it means that the project manager is able to get the work done, can control the project, can successfully negotiate for the resources needed, and can work with the customer and the other stakeholders in successfully accomplishing the goals of the project. In short, the project manager has enough depth of knowledge of the project to know whether the goals are being accomplished and knows how to keep the project moving toward a successful conclusion.

You can demonstrate your competence by learning everything possible about the project's objectives, goals, scope, specifications, and contractual requirements. No one should know more about the project than you. Otherwise, there would be no hope of successfully accomplishing the project goals, and a project vision could not be developed. Competence is a demonstration of knowledge in the form of judgment.

Forward-Looking

In project management, forward-looking means that the project manager can envision the end result. The project manager has to have a systems or holistic view of the project and be able to accomplish the project goals while meeting the company's strategic goals.

Most projects have a high degree of complexity. There can be hundreds of separate tasks, and all of them have to be integrated. Without the capacity to see how these tasks fit together to form a whole, the project manager may not meet the budget, schedule, and performance criteria.

To become forward-looking you have to develop a vision for the project, and the vision has to be centered around the customer's requirements. You don't have the flexibility of deciding how the end product will look or work separate from the customer's specifications. However, because you are the one person on the project team with a clear understanding of the goals, customer requirements, contractual requirements, company objectives, and how they all will be met, you can develop a vision from the amalgamation of this knowledge, the technical approach defined by these constraints, and the completed product as a result of putting all these elements together. It is this vision that the project manager develops and communicates to the team and all the stakeholders. The leader must exhibit that she or he has a vision and from it a defined direction for the project. A leader with an unclear direction or no direction won't be followed.

Inspiring

Without the ability to inspire a team to work together or to inspire ownership by each team member, the project will fail. After all, leadership is determined by the followers, because they will ultimately determine whether the project manager is a leader. A project manager must inspire the team to accept him or her as the leader, to get buy-in on the project, and to maintain a high morale level.

How do you inspire another? You have to be energetic and positive about the project. If a project is viewed as just a job, as it is in many organizations, the work tends to become mundane or routine. Every project is different. That is why project management cannot be reduced to routine. Consequently, a project manager needs to have a vision for the project and to communicate this vision to each team member. Inspiring the team with a vision means that the project manager is a cheerleader, a morale booster, and a champion for the project.

Five Management Practices and Ten Behavioral Commitments of Outstanding Leaders

Leadership qualities can be developed. Some leaders exhibit certain personality or behavioral characteristics that set them apart or make it easier to become what we typify as a leader. Understanding these leadership characteristics make it possible to develop into better, if not outstanding, leaders.

J.M. Kouzes and B.Z. Posner identified five management practices and ten behavioral commitments exhibited when leaders described their best leadership example.[5] I have adapted these practices and commitments, shown in Exhibit 4-2, to the project management environment.

Exhibit 4-2. Leadership practices and behavioral commitments of superior leaders.

Leadership Practices	Behavioral Commitments
Challenging the process	Search for opportunities.
	Experiment and take risks.
Inspiring a shared vision	Envision the future.
	Enlist others.
Enabling others to act	Foster collaboration.
	Strengthen others.
Modeling the way	Set the example.
	Plan small wins.
Encouraging the heart	Recognize individual contributions.
	Celebrate accomplishments.

Challenging the Process

Challenging processes is difficult for the project manager because most processes are directed by the organization's operating policies. However, it is not unusual for a project manager to circumvent a process if it is required to accomplish the goals of the project. The key is to work within the organizational framework for approval before violating an established process standard.

Search for Opportunities

The project manager is more constrained in challenging the process than is a functional manager. The customer has specific requirements that must be met, and the project manager violates the verbal or written contract if she or he unilaterally changes the project goals or specifications. That doesn't mean there aren't opportunities for challenging the process. Two obvious areas to seek opportunities for change and improvement come to mind immediately. One place is in the organization's process. Managing a project is difficult even when everything goes right, but invariably barriers to the project's progress occur because of outmoded or outdated policies and procedures. The project manager should constantly seek opportunities to force changes to the system to improve efficiency and team effectiveness. The second place for change opportunities is in the expected performance criteria of the project. Exceeding the customer's expectations is good business and good leadership.

Experiment and Take Risks

Experimentation and risk taking are anathema to project management. The constraints of budget, schedule, and performance have to be strenuously adhered to. Nevertheless, there are numerous occasions when hard decisions are needed about the technical approach, the type and skill level of resources, or whether to change direction if an approach isn't working. The easy way out is to avoid making these decisions or passing responsibility for them to a higher management level. A weak project manager either will not or cannot make a controversial or unpopular decision. However, the project team and the customer will soon view the person who can make these decisions as a leader and a credible manager.

Inspiring a Shared Vision

Every project manager has a vision of the project's path and successful conclusion. However, without inspiring the team to share—and support—that vision, the vision never becomes reality.

Envision the Future

The vision in project management is centered around the successful conclusion of the project, the customer's satisfaction with the product, and the fulfillment of corporate objectives. The project manager must clearly see the end result before the project is begun. Without a vision, a clear direction cannot be established. Without a vision, collaboration from others is not even possible.

Enlist Others

Having a vision is important, but without someone to share it with, it remains a vision without becoming a reality. Every superior leader talks about how a vision was made a reality by team work. Early enlistment of the project team, the customer, and all the stakeholders solidifies the parties at interest into a united whole, and the project will progress with greater support and fewer problems.

Enlisting others should be a priority for the project manager. It requires that he or she has a thorough understanding of the project's goals, scope, specifications, and objectives as well as an understanding of how the project fits into the business and strategic plans of the company. And it requires that the project manager conscientiously approach each party at interest and communicate the vision to them in such a way that they cannot but buy in to the vision. This requires skill, knowledge, and patience: skill in communicating the vision, knowledge about the project, and patience to continue to sell the vision when some of the parties at interest don't share the project manager's enthusiasm for the project.

Enabling Others to Act

Empowerment is an overworked word, but it is the appropriate word when trying to build a collaborative team spirit. If a project manager is foolhardy enough to believe that he or she can successfully complete a project's goals alone, then the project is doomed. But allowing the team to act when required, and to report the action and the results, not only ensures the project's success but engenders a team spirit that can work through any project problem.

Foster Collaboration

The surest path to failure is to ignore building a collaborative team spirit. Since followers define leadership, it is incumbent on the project manager to forge relationships and to foster and encourage collaboration among all the team members.

Amazingly, some people still believe in management by intimidation, so they think that a team can be bullied into top performance. Even if a project is completed by utilizing the intimidation management method, the toll on the team is horrendous, and the long-term costs to the organization are stiff in terms of morale and employee retainability. On the other hand, management that is too laid-back is equally devastating. Collaboration—fostering a cooperative spirit toward achieving common goals—is in the middle of these two extremes. It is the first step in enabling team members to function at the peak of their capability.

Strengthen Others

Strengthening others is daunting for some project managers because it appears to be giving up control or power. When a team member is enabled by giving him or her responsibility and authority to perform designated functions, the individual and the team are strengthened. Project managers also discover that rather than losing control by passing down responsibility and authority, they actually gain more control. Enabling team members fosters collaboration, which translates into power for the project manager. Real power in a leader is stronger if the power is bestowed by the followers than if it results from the position. Hence, everyone gains.

Strengthening the team member strengthens the team and the project manager—an unstoppable combination for achieving project goals.

Modeling the Way

The great dichotomy of leadership is that it cannot be taught, but it can be learned. That is to say, we can read about leadership, study leadership, and understand the characteristics of good leaders, but we become leaders by example. It is only by understanding ourselves and demonstrating our leadership qualities that we become leaders. Modeling requires that we demonstrate our leadership, and then others will follow.

Set the Example

Leading by example should be the self-evident mode of management. Nevertheless, all too often we find people in leadership positions who think the way to manage is to bully or cajole or otherwise intimidate. Usually this type of behavior is characteristic of an insecure person. Knowing that helps us to deal with the person, but how should we act as leaders?

Leading by example isn't easy. It requires being "on" more often perhaps than we would like. Leading by example means being consistent, being willing to do what you ask others to do, and fostering and practicing high ethical standards. In short, it means being and acting the way you want your team to be and act.

Plan Small Wins

People and teams react positively when they win. Planning a project so that the team works toward achievable goals is a natural for project management. Projects are generally too complex and run too long to plan in large phases. To be sure, there has to be an overall plan, a master plan, which clearly establishes milestones, goals, and schedules. However, a good project manager will use what is sometimes referred to as a sliding planning window (see Exhibit 4-3). This concept breaks the project into small, manageable segments— project phases, discrete time lengths, milestone-

Exhibit 4-3. Sliding planning window.

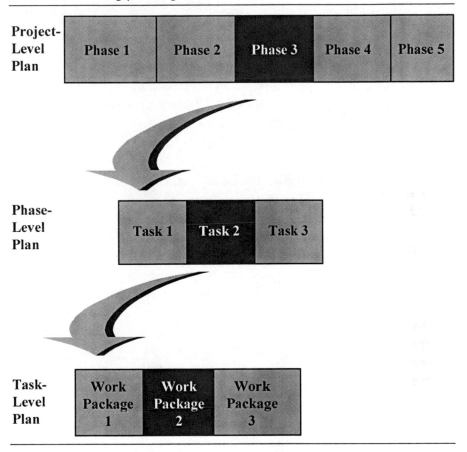

to-milestone increments or a combination of these—that are thoroughly planned. How the segments are defined is not as important. What is important is that the segment be long enough to offer a challenge but short enough to visualize and achieve an end to it. These discrete wins will serve to build team morale and will build a collaborative spirit among all who are involved with the project.

Encouraging the Heart

Behavioral theorists claim that self-actualization is a primary goal of every individual—that is, everyone wants to feel a sense of accomplishment and be recognized for it. Wise project managers are conscientious about acknowledging accomplishments and doing so in public.

Recognize Individual Contributions

Every person wants and needs to be acknowledged. Small acknowledgments of the good work performed result in large performance boosts. Superior leaders give credit where credit is due and reap enormous benefits in the form of loyalty and even devotion.

Acknowledging performance demonstrates a caring spirit. Individuals and teams react positively when they have proof that the leader cares how they perform. The reverse is also true. If a leader doesn't acknowledge performance, the individual feels the leader doesn't care, and his or her performance will deteriorate.

Acknowledging performance is important, but just as important is how it is acknowledged. Performance should be rewarded, with the level of reward commensurate with the accomplishment. Sometimes it is sufficient just to acknowledge by name and deed the accomplishment in a staff meeting. Some accomplishments are big enough and important enough to reward with a dinner for two, a paid weekend at a nearby resort, or a cash bonus. Many companies give their project managers the authority to make such awards. Be sure you check the policies on this at your company, and if none exist, suggest they be implemented.

Celebrate Accomplishments

Finally, every leader needs to make it possible for the whole team to celebrate accomplishments. The celebrations often will be spontaneous when one person or the team accomplishes something extraordinary or unexpectedly. Perhaps someone makes a breakthrough in the technical approach that had bogged down the project.

Project teams should also have scheduled celebration activities. Special holidays are obvious choices, but just regularly scheduled events will show the team that the leader cares. It also bonds the team. The feeling that everyone is working together develops, and pride of ownership of the project and the pride of belonging to the team will build morale and foster collaboration.

Summary

There are two leadership extremes: authoritarian or autocratic, which is more concerned with the task, and democratic or egalitarian, which is oriented toward relationships. In general, the autocratic style works well only in special situations. For instance, the military is built on the autocratic style of leadership because of the nature and rapidity with which orders have to be given and unthinking reaction results. In other work environments, the autocratic style tends to create tension, dislike for the supervisor, and a significant reduction in performance. The democratic style of leadership, on the other hand, generally leads to high morale and high performance.

The Technical Tools

CHAPTER 5

The Work Breakdown Structure

The project WBS is the heart . . . the framework
on which the project is built.

—S. E. STEPHANOU AND M. M. OBRADOVITCH
Project Management, System Development, and Productivity

The work breakdown structure (WBS) is perhaps the most useful tool of project management. It takes a variety of forms and serves a variety of purposes. When done correctly, the WBS is the basis for project planning, scheduling, budgeting, and controlling.

In spite of its value, though, many writers give little attention to the WBS and scarcely make mention of its use.[1] A WBS is not the only way to plan a project, and as long as some disciplined and detailed method for planning is used, the project can be successfully managed. However, the WBS is such a fundamental requirement of many customers and can be used to such powerful advantage that a project manager would be wise to make developing a WBS his or her first priority.

One of the reasons that the WBS is not more widely used is that the concept is not well understood. Even writers who espouse the virtues of WBS do not clearly explain the elements of it and how to develop one. The fact is that the literature is vague, often inconsistent, and usually incomplete about WBS development. It is not surprising that the WBS is too difficult and too frustrating to use, but this does not have to be the case.

Developing a WBS is not particularly easy, especially for complex projects. This chapter provides a simple approach that will facilitate the process.

What Is a WBS?

The WBS is the basis of a plan for the successful accomplishment of project objectives. It is a structured way of decomposing a project into its various components: hardware, software, services, documentation, labor, testing, delivery, and installation. In short, the WBS is a formalized way of reducing the project into successively lower levels of greater detail.

The project decomposition should continue only to the level that is needed to identify the task or subtask as a *work package,* a natural subdivision of a cost account. It is a job assignment that is identifiable with a person, a job, or a budget number and is where the actual project work is accomplished. The work package can occur anywhere below the first level, but usually occurs at the fifth level. *Levels* refer to the successively lower tiers of detail beginning with the project name as the first level. The WBS almost never needs to be developed below the fifth level.

Think of WBS development as similar to a flowcharting process, except that we start with the project and decompose it into progressively smaller elements until the desired level of detail is achieved. Flowcharting usually starts with the most detailed or basic element and charts the steps toward the end or final product. The thought process for both, however, is linear and requires that each successive step be sequential, logical, and at the appropriate level of detail. If the WBS is viewed in this manner, it is easier to identify the project components.

The two most common forms for WBS presentation are the indented and the graphical or tree form. The *indented* format, shown in Exhibit 5-1, derives its name from the practice of indenting each project level to delineate between them and to identify each of the

Exhibit 5-1. Indented WBS format.

1.0 Project or Contract Name
   1.1 Major Project Subsystem 1
      1.1.1 Task 1
         1.1.1.1 Subtask 1
            1.1.1.1.1 Work Package 1

      1.1.2 Task 2
         1.1.2.1 Subtask 1
         1.1.2.2 Subtask 2
            1.1.2.2.1 Work Package 1
            1.1.2.2.2 Work Package 2

   1.2 Major Project Subsystem 2
      1.2.1 Task 1
         1.2.1.1 Subtask 1
            1.2.1.1.1 Work Package 1
               1.2.1.1.1.1 Components

   1.3 Major Project Subsystem 3

---

levels. It is the most popular WBS format—the one used by all the project management software packages and it is required when specified in Requests for Proposals or Requests for Quotes. The *graphical* format, shown in Exhibit 5-2, resembles a traditional organizational chart. It is an effective format for those who work better from visual presentations of data. However, it does take a lot of space to develop, particularly for large, complex projects.

Analysis of the Work Breakdown Structure

The WBS is the single most important project management tool. With a completely defined WBS, every other project management tool can be developed. It completely describes the project's scope—if it isn't in the work breakdown structure, it is not in the project.

Exhibit 5-2. Graphical WBS format.

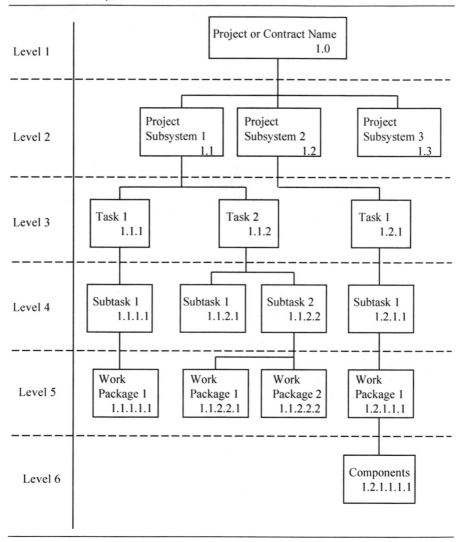

The WBS Levels

The project or the contract name is always the first level of the WBS. (Exhibit 5-3 shows the format with explanations.) In project management literature, level 1 is often called the program, with level 2 called the project. However, this nomenclature is confusing

Exhibit 5-3. Indented WBS format with explanations.

Numbering Element	Description	Levels	Type of Format
1.0	Project or Contract Name	1	Managerial
1.1	Major Project Subsystem	2	Managerial
1.1.1	Task	3	Managerial
1.1.1.1	Subtask	4	Technical
1.1.1.1.1	Work package	5	Technical
1.1.1.1.1.1	Components	6	Technical

because the term *program* generally is interpreted to mean a collection of several projects with similar characteristics. Except in rare cases, though, a project manager will be concerned with only one discrete project at a time, and each project will have its own WBS. Therefore, to eliminate the semantic confusion created by using *program,* always designate the name of the project as the level 1 entry in the WBS. Then there will never be any doubt about what levels 1 and 2 should be.

Level 2 is composed of the major subsystems of the project—complete entities or sections of the project. The level 2 entries for an automobile design project, for example, would be the engine, the chassis, the interior, and the body, all of them complete subsystems of the automobile. Or suppose the project is to design, develop, and build a human centrifuge training system. Then the project name (level 1) of the WBS would be Human Centrifuge Trainer Contract. The major subsystems are the training device itself, technical support data (e.g., engineering data, administrative reports, logistics reports), the project management function, logistics support, and field services such as maintenance. Each of these subsystems will be a level 2 entry of the WBS.

Each level 2 entry can also consist of one or more major task activities. For instance, under the training device there are systems engineering, hardware, electrical, and mechanical design, and software design. These are designated as level 3 activities, each of which can be decomposed into several more discrete activities, and so on until the desired level of detail is achieved.

For example, the level 3 activity of mechanical design might be divided into several subtasks, such as the support axis design, cockpit shell design, and cockpit interior design. These level 3 activity subtasks are entered into the WBS at level 4. Continuing the process, the level 4 activity of support axis design now can be expanded to a level where actual work can be assigned. That is, discrete work packages for preparing engineering drawings, analyzing structural strength, manufacturing structural members, and so on can be assigned to particular individuals or groups. The work package is level 5 and usually the lowest level ever required. Level 6 deals with components such as screws, computer chips, or other off-the-shelf items that are needed but not usually tracked by the project manager.

Exhibit 5-4 shows a small portion of the human centrifuge example. The actual WBS from which the example is taken is five pages in length. Note in Exhibit 5-4 that some of the activities are expanded to level 5, while others are expanded to only level 4. There are two points to remember from this: (1) All activities in a WBS do not have to be expanded to the same level, and (2) it is not required to go to level 5 to define a work package. Often, an activity only has to be expanded to level 4 or even level 3. The idea is to use the WBS as a tool to define the project work, and the activities should be expanded only to the level required to clearly do that.

The WBS Numbering System

Project management literature often does not adequately explain the importance of numbering the project activities. The numbering system can be numeric, alphabetic, or a combination of the two. The important thing to remember is that the first number is the number assigned to the project, and it is used by most companies as a means of tracking the project's costs and progress with the company's accounting and scheduling system. The first number does not have to be 1.0. Let's say the human centrifuge project

Exhibit 5-4. Section of a work breakdown structure for a human centrifuge contract.

1.0 Human Centrifuge Trainer Contract
  1.1 Training Device
    1.1.1 Systems Engineering
      1.1.1.1 Write Systems Engineering Management Plan
      1.1.1.2 Develop Systems Detail Design Specification
        1.1.1.2.1 Perform System Requirements Analysis
      1.1.1.3 Develop Hardware System Design Specifications
      1.1.1.4 Develop Software System Design Specifications
      1.1.1.5 Do Reliability/Maintainability Engineering
        1.1.1.5.1 Write Safety Engineering Plan
        1.1.1.5.2 Write Human Factors Engineering Plan
        1.1.1.5.3 Write Reliability Engineering Plan
        1.1.1.5.4 Write Maintainability Engineering Plan
        1.1.1.5.6 Perform Preliminary Stress Analysis
        1.1.1.5.7 Write EMC/EMI Engineering Plan
      1.1.1.6 Develop Support Facility Design Specifications
        1.1.1.6.1 Determine Systems Control Methods
        1.1.1.6.2 Develop Hardware & Software Interfaces Plan
        1.1.1.6.3 Prepare Site Plans and Facility Drawings
        1.1.1.6.4 Perform Electric Power & Duty Cycle Analyses
    1.1.2 Hardware, Electrical, and Mechanical Design
      1.1.2.1 Design Student Station
        1.1.2.1.1 Design Support Axis
        1.1.2.1.2 Design Cockpit Shell
        1.1.2.1.3 Design Cockpit Interior
    1.1.3 Detailed Software Design
      1.1.3.1 Develop System Program
      1.1.3.2 Develop Simulation Program
        1.1.3.2.1 Write Executive Program
        1.1.3.2.2 Write G Loading Control Algorithms
      1.1.3.3 Develop Instruction on Control Programs
        1.1.3.3.1 Write Lessons for General System Controls

        1.1.3.3.2 Write Lessons for Trainer Mode Controls

        1.1.3.3.3 Write Lessons for Emergency Controls

      1.1.3.4 Write Lesson Database Programs

        1.1.3.4.1 Develop and Write Beginner Scenario

        1.1.3.4.2 Develop and Write Advanced Scenario

        1.1.3.4.3 Develop and Write Custom Scenario

      1.1.3.5 Develop Utility Program

        1.1.3.5.1 Write Computer Diagnostics Program

        1.1.3.5.2 Write Operations Readiness Tests

        1.1.3.5.3 Write Real-Time Interface Diagnostics
Program

    1.2 Project Management

      1.2.1 Project Manager

        1.2.1.1 Project Engineer

        1.2.1.2 Cost Analyst

        1.2.1.3 Clerical Support

---

could be the fifty-first project of 2006. Someone in the company who tracks projects might assign the number 5105 to the project so that it both has a unique designator (51) and shows how many projects were started to date in 2006. Hence, the level 1 entry becomes *5105.0 Human Centrifuge Trainer Contract.* A level 2 entry would then be 5105.1, and so on. Every other digit place can also have unique designators composed of numeric, alphabetic, or a combination in the scheme. For instance, the designator 5105.A.14.20 is interpreted as the twentieth subtask of the fourteenth task under the major project component A in project 5105. You can quickly grasp why careful attention to the numbering scheme is important for tracking and accounting procedures and why a consistent numbering hierarchy be practiced. Many writers correctly identify the project name as the first WBS level but then start the numbering system with the second level. In these cases, they also do not indent the second level, so that our example would be shown as:

Human Centrifuge Trainer Contract

1.0   Training Device

1.1 Systems Engineering
    1.1.1 Systems Engineering Management Plan

1.2 Hardware, Electrical, and Mechanical Design

The problem with this procedure is that the "Training Device" and "Hardware, Electrical, and Mechanical Design" entries appear in the first-level positions, which is inconsistent with conventional practice. This numbering scheme, therefore, confuses the budget and tracking systems. To be consistent with the convention and to facilitate tracking, the project name should *always* be designated as the first-level entry. In so doing, there will be only one first-level entry for each project. In addition, anyone can immediately identify an activity's level, even when taken out of context, because all succeeding levels after level 1 are identified by the number of digit places. For instance, we know the entry *1.1.2.1 Student Station* from Exhibit 5-4 is a fourth-level activity because there are four digit positions in its number.

Types of WBS Activity Entries

The first three levels in the WBS are typically managerial levels (see Exhibit 5-3). That is, each level represents a management level and not a level at which the work is actually accomplished. The third level, "Task," usually represents a task leader position—the person responsible for supervising the task. Remembering those designations will facilitate decomposing the project into lower, and more detailed, levels.

The last three levels are where the work is actually accomplished. The subtask level might be composed of several work packages, so level 4 might be the system integration level. For instance, one of the level 4 entries might be to design databases for various scenarios in our example. One of the databases might be for a beginning pilot, another might be more advanced, including air combat maneuvers, a third might be customized for the particular user. Hence, each of these separate databases is developed by a person or team, and then they are integrated into a central computer system.

Level 5, the work package level, is usually the lowest level of detail ever needed in a project WBS because the next level, level 6, describes such things as the production of computer chips and screws that do not need to be tracked.

WBS Element Description

One final word about how to describe these entries might help in the WBS development. If the first three levels are described by noun words and the last three entries are described by action words, it will be clear what type of activity goes into each level. In Exhibit 5-4, note that beginning with level 4, the technical levels, each entry begins with an action word denoting what sort of work is actually accomplished.

WBS Uses

The WBS is a multipurpose tool. Some important uses are as a basis for assigning task responsibility, project costing, network analysis, scheduling, and project control.

How to Assign Task Responsibility Using the WBS

Assigning task responsibility is one of the most important uses of the WBS. The completed WBS will expose all the component parts of the project down to a workable level of detail. Once this is done, it will be self-evident who should do each piece of work and who should supervise each effort. The project manager, in coordination with the appropriate functional managers, will develop a task responsibility matrix, assigning a name to each of the WBS elements. This task responsibility matrix then shows at a glance who is responsible for every piece of work on the project.

Project Costing

The second most important use of the WBS is for project costing. It is virtually impossible to estimate the cost of a project by viewing the project as a whole. Clearly the project has to be reduced to smaller elements until the cost of each element can be determined. As the cost of each smaller element is determined, the costs are "rolled up" to finally obtain one number for the whole project. The WBS is the perfect tool for this purpose because it decomposes the project into sufficient detail so that the cost of each element can be determined.

I always include the project management function as a line item entry (1.2 in Exhibit 5-4) in the WBS. Every other entry includes the labor cost of the tasks. The project manager, though, and any other project office staff spread their labor costs across the entire project. That is, the project manager doesn't just work on a task. He or she is supervising the entire project. Therefore, rather than try to apportion the project manager's time to every single task, it is much easier to include a separate WBS entry for this function and then provide a total cost for the estimated project duration.

Network Analysis

The WBS provides the basis for development of the *network analysis*, a method of representing the activities or tasks of a project by a series of lines and nodes to show the interrelations of these various activities. Several important pieces of information can be derived from a network analysis; the critical path, which is the path that takes the longest to traverse (the critical path determines the minimum schedule length with a given resource allocation); early start and finish times for each activity; and the amount of slack time the project manager can expect for each activity. (See Chapter 6 for a discussion of how to develop and interpret a network.)

Scheduling

Scheduling the project activities is difficult unless there is a clear understanding of all the activity requirements and how each of the activities relates to the others. For instance, a number of activities cannot begin until one or more preceding activities have been completed. Without a detailed breakdown of the project, it is easy to overlook these interrelationships or to overlook certain activities completely. The WBS is a way to analyze the project's activities from the perspective of creating schedules that will have the requisite beginning and ending points for each activity while observing their dependency hierarchies.

Project Control

Controlling a project requires a complete understanding of the project's activities: who is responsible for each, how they interrelate, how much each element should cost, and how long each activity should take for completion. The WBS is the basis of each of the tools already discussed, which, in turn, are the tools that the project manager uses to track and control the project.

Summary

This chapter has presented a simple approach to the development of a WBS, a powerful tool but one that is not clearly described in the literature. Although WBS development is not easy, following the approach and the guidelines provides a workable model for the project manager. Some important guidelines for WBS development are:

- The project name or contract name is always the first-level entry.
- There will be only one first-level entry for each project.
- The first three levels of a WBS are managerial levels.
- Technical project work usually occurs at the fourth and fifth levels.
- The lowest level of any project is usually the fifth level.
- Major subdivisions do not have to be reduced to the same level.

When the WBS is correctly developed and used, it becomes the basis for planning, scheduling, budgeting, and controlling.

CHAPTER 6

Network Analysis

Often the parts are not the same as the whole—
look at the entire picture before you act.

—Robin T. Peterson
Managing Without Blinders

Prior to 1950, no project tracking or controlling methods adequately showed the interdependencies of project activities. In the 1950s, this all changed when the Project Evaluation Review Technique (PERT) was developed by Lockheed and Booz Allen Hamilton as an evaluation and tracking tool for the U.S. Navy's Polaris missile program. Since then, other network analysis tools have been developed to compensate for shortcomings or disadvantages of the PERT method or to provide specialized capabilities that PERT does not possess. Although there are several network analysis tools available, the three most common ones are the PERT, the critical path method (CPM), and the precedence diagram method (PDM). This chapter discusses each method and demonstrates how each one is used to analyze a project.

Using Logic Diagrams and Networks

A logic diagram is simply a diagram showing the major elements of a task and their logical relationship to each other. Exhibit 6-1

Exhibit 6-1. A logic diagram for a man getting dressed and eating breakfast.

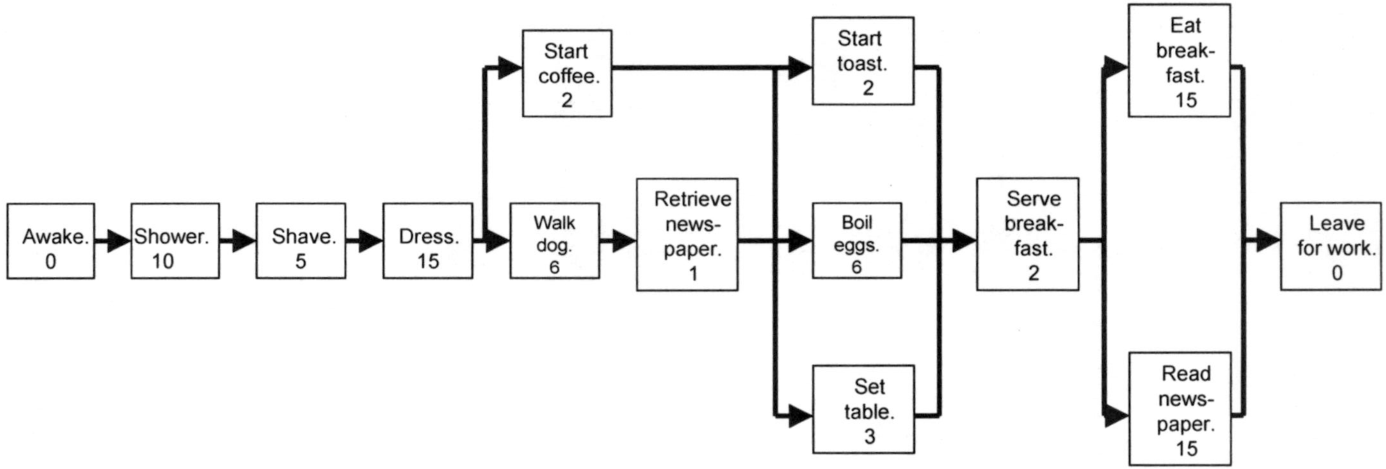

Awake. 0

Shower. 10

Shave. 5

Dress. 15

Start coffee. 2

Walk dog. 6

Retrieve news-paper. 1

Start toast. 2

Boil eggs. 6

Set table. 3

Serve break-fast. 2

Eat break-fast. 15

Read news-paper. 15

Leave for work. 0

(Time in minutes)

shows a logic diagram that describes the process of getting dressed in the morning. The boxes, called *nodes,* depict the tasks that have to be accomplished, while the arrows, sometimes called *arcs,* show the relationship of the tasks to each other and the sequence in which they have to be accomplished.

There are two ways to construct a network: One shows the activities on the nodes (AON), and the second shows the activities on the arrows (AOA). If the activities are shown on the nodes, then the arrows have no substance; that is, they simply show interdependencies and sequences but have no duration or resources attached to them. However, if the activities are shown on the arrows, then the nodes have no substance. They just indicate the beginning or ending points for the activities.

The PERT and CPM are both AOA networks. The PDM is an AON analysis method. Neither the AOA nor the AON methods are particularly difficult to construct once the basic principles of construction are understood. The analysis of each type is exactly the same. However, the AOA method does have the disadvantage that dummy activities can occur. A dummy activity is one that places an additional constraint on one or more of the other activities but has no duration or resources associated with it. For example, suppose task C is *dependent* upon task A for a key design drawing. Task C, then, is constrained by the technical activity of task A, and cannot start until task A is completed. Suppose also that task B is *independent* of both task A and task C. That means task B can begin simultaneously with task A, and task C can begin regardless of when task B is completed. Suppose, though, that you plan to use some of the task B team members to accomplish task C. Task C then becomes constrained by task B, but not because of a technical dependency between the two. This relationship (the dummy activity) between the two tasks is real, but the "activity" of the relationship requires no actual expenditure of resources, and no work is involved in getting from one task to the other. Nevertheless, task C cannot begin until task B is finished. The dummy activity will be completely described and demonstrated in due course, but since this is a characteristic of the AOA–type network and adds a small degree of complexity to the description of it, we shall consider the slightly simpler AON network first. AON networks do not have dummy activities and therefore are somewhat easier to construct.

AON Networks (The Precedence Diagram Method)

AON networks describe a project with the nodes representing the activities or work units. Usually each node represents the lowest level of the WBS, so work unit relationships can be assessed. The network can be drawn showing any level of the WBS, depending on the level of detail needed and the desired result. For instance, if the project is a fairly long and complex one, it may be useful to do a high-level network analysis to determine the overall schedule and when certain resources might be needed. More detail can be obtained from analyzing the complete project or discrete phases of it. The point is that a network analysis can be performed at various levels of detail over the entire project or over individual tasks, depending on the information needed.

One of the major advantages of the PDM or AON is that it can accommodate different activity sequencing, and it can account for lead and lag times. For instance, the AOA method requires that activities be sequenced from the finish of one activity to the start of another. In contrast, the PDM allows the use of finish-to-start, start-to-start, start-to-finish, and finish-to-finish sequencing. Also, the PDM allows the use of lead and lag times if needed. For instance, if one activity is to pour a concrete floor and another is to erect a building frame, the frame cannot be built until the concrete floor is dry. So, although the concrete floor is poured and that part of the activity is complete, we might need to add a lag time of five days to allow the floor to dry before starting the next activity. The concept of alternative sequencing and lag is shown in Exhibit 6-2.

Basic Network Construction

The WBS is the most important tool of the project manager. From it, all the other tools can be derived. The network is an example of a tool derived from WBS information.

The network is a logic diagram of the interdependencies of the

Exhibit 6-2. Alternative task sequencing.

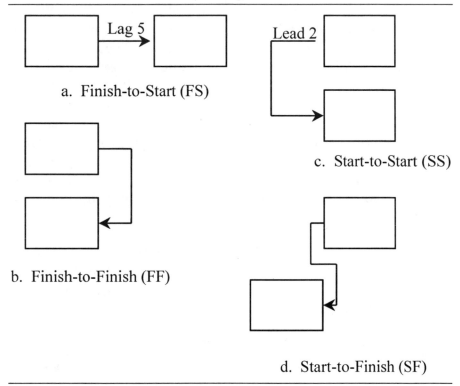

a. Finish-to-Start (FS)

b. Finish-to-Finish (FF)

c. Start-to-Start (SS)

d. Start-to-Finish (SF)

various project tasks. The WBS is an object- or service-oriented depiction of the project with the tasks decomposed into increasingly greater levels of detail until a level is reached at which work can be assigned. This level is called the *work package*.

Once the WBS is developed, three questions have to be answered for each activity in the project in order to construct the network:

1. What activities must be completed before this activity can start? These are the *predecessors*.
2. What activities follow this activity? These are the *successors*.
3. What activities can be accomplished independently or in parallel with this activity?

The first step in constructing a network is to identify every activity and each of its predecessors. The easiest way of doing this is to construct a table and, with the help of the project team, analyze the project WBS to determine the predecessors. The analysis that was done for Exhibit 6-1 is recorded in Exhibit 6-3. Exhibit 6-3 also has added estimated duration times for each of the activities and an alphabetic descriptor for each. The alphabetic descriptor is used instead of the full description of the activity to reduce the clutter on the network. Networks can be complex enough without adding activity descriptions.

Once the predecessors are determined, the network can be drawn as shown in Exhibit 6-4. Some important points to note about the network are that:

- Arrows indicate the direction of the work flow.
- The nodes contain the alphabetic identifier and the duration.
- Every node has either a successor or predecessor or both, except the beginning and ending ones.

Exhibit 6-3. Analysis of getting dressed and eating breakfast.

Activity	Alphabetic Designator	Immediate Predecessor(s)	Activity Duration (in minutes)
Awake.	a	—	0
Shower.	b	a	10
Shave.	c	b	5
Dress.	d	c	15
Start coffee.	e	d	2
Walk dog.	f	d	6
Retrieve newspaper.	g	f	1
Start toast.	h	g	2
Boil eggs.	i	g	3
Set table.	j	g	3
Serve breakfast.	k	h, i, j	2
Eat breakfast.	l	k	15
Read newspaper.	m	k	15
Leave for work.	n	l, m	0

Exhibit 6-4. AON (precedence diagram) for getting dressed and eating breakfast.

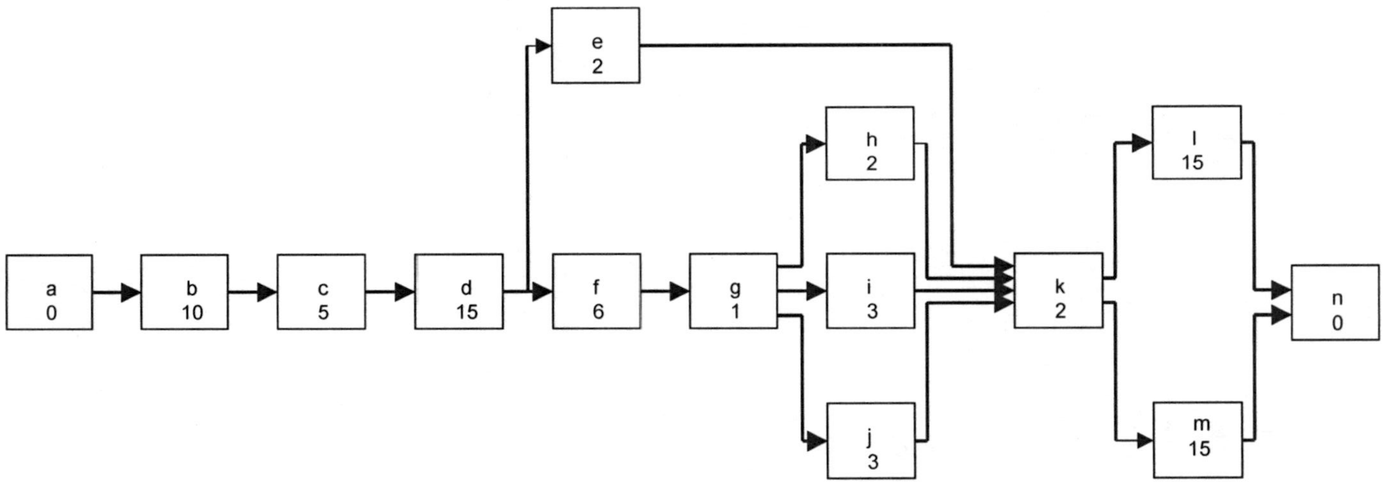

- It is not necessary to draw a dummy activity to describe the project.

AOA Network Construction (The PERT Method)

Activity-on-the-arrow construction follows the same general procedure as the AON in that the initial steps are to construct the figure shown in the Exhibit 6-5. An additional constraint in the construction of an AOA network is necessary, however. Each activity must be represented by its own arrow, and only one arrow can be drawn between the same two nodes. This situation gives rise to the possibility of a dummy activity. Exhibit 6-5 demonstrates how to construct a dummy activity when two activities occur between the same two nodes or when a nontechnical dependency exists between the two.

In Exhibit 6-5A, two activities, a and b, emanate from node 1, and both terminate at node 2. However, the rule of network construction is that only one arrow can be drawn between the same two nodes. To avoid this situation, a third node, node 3, is drawn as the terminus of activity b. Then a dummy activity is drawn from node 3 to node 2. The dummy activity is always shown as a dashed line to distinguish it from normal project activities. Another important characteristic of the dummy activity is that it has no substance; that is, no resources and no duration are assigned to it. The dummy construction is simply a way of indicating

Exhibit 6-5. Constructing dummy activities.

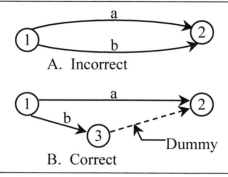

A. Incorrect

B. Correct

an additional constraint that has to be met prior to any activity beginning at node 2.

The numbers within the nodes of an AON network have no significance other than to identify the node. It is a convenient way of keeping track of activities in the network. The order of numbering the nodes is generally unimportant. However, the convention is to number them beginning at the left of the network (the start) and progressing to the end. In the event of parallel activities, the nodes are usually numbered from the top to the bottom.

The network for the getting-dressed example as it is drawn in the AOA format is shown in Exhibit 6-6. Notice the differences between Exhibit 6-4 and 6-6. Although the two networks look similar, there are some distinct differences. First, the duration times and the activity designators are written on the arrows of Exhibit 6-6 and on the nodes of Exhibit 6-4. But, most important in the AOA network, there has to be a dummy activity drawn from nodes 8 and 9 to node 10, and from nodes 12 and 13 to node 14 to show the additional constraint on activity g. We did not have to indicate a dummy in Exhibit 6-4 since arrows in the AON networks only show sequences and constraints and have no substance. Since the arrows in the AOA network have values associated with them, we had to invent the activity. Remember that the dummy itself has no duration, resources, or anything else associated with it. It just shows the added constraint that activity g can not begin before activities d and f are finished.

Estimating Activity Duration

One of the big challenges in constructing a network is estimating the activity duration. If a project is very similar to numerous other previous projects in the company, then duration can be estimated with good accuracy from experience and historical data. In the construction industry, for example, the various phases in building a house can be predicted with great accuracy. When the project manager approaches those individuals responsible for each task, they can readily assign a duration estimate. What happens, though, in a research-and-development project where the project is break-

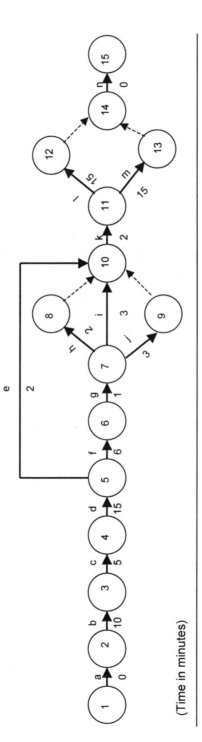

Exhibit 6-6. AOA network of getting dressed and eating breakfast.

(Time in minutes)

ing new ground and is completely new to the company? How can the project manager estimate duration and account for the risk associated with the uncertainty in a project?

It was this problem that led to the development of PERT. The Polaris missile program was so complex, and there was so much new technology associated with it, that a new tool for analyzing the project had to be developed. A key difference in the PERT analysis from other network analysis methods is that the duration of each activity is statistically derived. That is, each activity duration is determined using three times: the most optimistic estimate, the most pessimistic estimate, and the most likely estimate. Then apply the following formula:

$$T_e = \frac{a + 4m + b}{6}$$

Where: a = most optimistic time
b = most pessimistic time
m = most likely time
T_e = estimate duration

The duration time, T_e, is calculated. An example of this process is shown in Exhibit 6-7.

T_e for the first activity, system design, is calculated by using the previous formula. Substituting the values for a, b, and m, we get:

$$T_e = \frac{6 + (4 \times 8.25) + 9}{6}$$

$$T_e = \frac{48}{6}$$

$$T_e = 8 \text{ weeks}$$

The T_e for all subsequent activities is calculated in the same way. It is the T_e value that is used as the duration time on the activity arrows in the PERT network.

Exhibit 6–7. Estimated durations using PERT analysis.

Activity	Optimistic Times (weeks)	Most Likely Times (weeks)	Pessimistic Times (weeks)	T_e
System design.	6	8.25	9	8
Procure hardware components.	4	4.75	7	5
Assemble.	2	5.5	6	5
Test hardware system.	2	2	2	2
Develop software.	10	13.25	15	13
Test software.	3	4	5	4
Integrate hardware and software.	2	3.75	7	4
Test integrated system.	2	3	4	3
Deliver system.	1	1	1	1
Install system.	2	2	2	2

The PERT formula describes the beta distribution, or the well-known bell curve, shown in Exhibit 6-8. Most of us are very familiar with the bell curve and that statistically approximately 68 percent of the samples of a population will fall between -1σ and $+1\sigma$, where σ represents the standard deviation. Similarly, approximately 95 percent of the sampled data will fall between -2σ and $+2\sigma$, and a little over 99 percent will fall between -3σ and $+3\sigma$. What many people do *not* realize is that the area under the beta distribution curve from -3σ to $+1\sigma$ contains about 85 percent of the samples, from -3σ to $+2\sigma$ contains 99 percent, and from -3σ to $+3\sigma$ contains nearly 100 percent of the samples.

Given that the formula for T_e is actually an average number, the duration calculated from the formula is the mean of the bell

Exhibit 6-8. The bell curve and standard deviation.

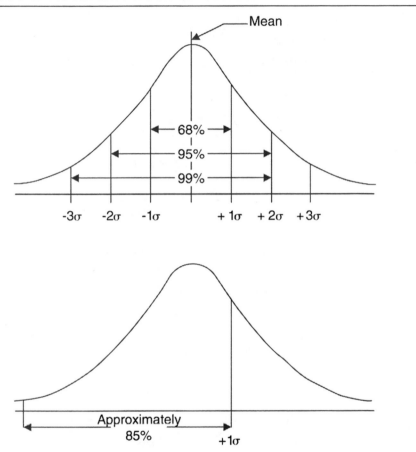

curve, or at the 50 percent mark. Hence, there is only a 50 percent probability that a task can be finished before or on the T_e calculated by the PERT formula. In order to have an 85 percent chance of completing the task on or before T_e, the duration time has to be increased by one standard deviation; a 99 percent probability requires increasing the T_e by two standard deviations, and so on.

Standard deviation is not difficult to calculate. The optimistic and pessimistic times used for the T_e calculation are also used to calculate standard deviation where standard deviation, σ, is given by:

$$\sigma = \frac{b - a}{6}$$

where: b = pessimistic time
a = optimistic time

Hence, for our example from Exhibit 6-7, the standard deviation for the system design activity is:

$$\sigma = \frac{9 - 6}{6}$$

$$\sigma = .5$$

Therefore, to ensure that we have a 100 percent probability of finishing the system design activity, we must add 3 σ's to the calculated Te. Hence, the duration time for this activity then becomes:

$$T_e = 8.83 + 3 \times \sigma$$
$$= 8.83 + 3 \times .5$$
$$= 8.83 + 1.5$$
$$= 10.33 \text{ weeks}$$

The beauty of the PERT analysis is that it provides us with a way to account for risk in task duration estimation.

Calculating the Critical Path and the Project Duration

The critical path in a network is defined as the longest path from the beginning of the network to the end. A path is a track defined by following the arrows from node to node, from network start to network finish, in the direction of the arrows. Suppose we have the project described by Exhibit 6-9. Using these duration times for the activities and their predecessors, we can construct the PERT network diagram shown in Exhibit 6-10. The various paths in this project are indicated on the graphic.

In order to determine what the critical path is for the network

Exhibit 6-9. PERT durations for a generic project.

Activity	Predecessor(s)	Times (days)			
		a	m	b	T_e
a	—	6	7.5	9	7.5
b	a	4	5.0	6	5.0
c	a	2	5.5	6	5.0
d	a	10	14.75	15	14.0
e	b	3	4.0	5	4.0
f	c, d	2	2.75	5	3.0
g	d	5	6.0	7	6.0
h	e, f, g	4	5.75	9	6.0

Exhibit 6-10. Paths of a network.

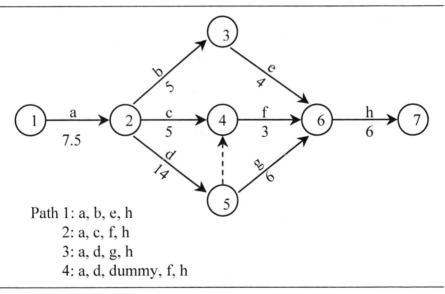

Path 1: a, b, e, h
    2: a, c, f, h
    3: a, d, g, h
    4: a, d, dummy, f, h

in Exhibit 6-10, we calculate the earliest occurrence time (EOT) at each of the nodes. The EOT is the earliest time that a succeeding activity can start. Looking at Exhibit 6-10, we see that the earliest time that activities b, c, and d can start is at the end of 7.5 days, because it takes 7.5 days to accomplish the work of activity a. The earliest that activity e can begin is at the end of 12.5 days (start of activity b is at 8.5 days, and it takes 5 days to accomplish the activity). The process continues in this fashion to the end of the network. However, notice at node 6 that there will be four EOT possibilities coming into node 6. It we look at the path a-b-e, the EOT at node 6 will be 16.5 days; path a-c-f yields an EOT of 15.5 days; path a-d-dummy-f yields an EOT of 24.5 days; and, path a-d-g yields an EOT of 28.5 days. The correct EOT to use is 28.5 days, because the rule is that all activities have to be completed before the following activity or activities can begin.

Hence, if we choose any EOT of less duration than 28.5 days, one or more of the other activities could not be completed. With the EOT at node 6 being 28.5 days, getting to node 8 will require 33.5 days. This number, 33.5 days, is the estimated average duration required to accomplish this project. Remember that there is only a 50 percent probability of completing the project within 33.5 days. To ensure a 100 percent probability of success, we have to calculate the standard deviation of the critical path.

Calculating the standard deviation of the critical path is not quite as simple as adding the individual activity σ's; it requires another formula.

To calculate the standard deviation of the critical path (described in the next section) requires another formula.

$$SD_{\text{Critical Path}} = \sqrt{\sigma_1^2 + \sigma_2^2 + \sigma_3^2 \cdots \sigma_n^2}$$

Where: $SD_{\text{Critical Path}}$ = standard deviation
σ_n^2 = standard deviation squared for each critical path task.

But first we have to determine which the critical path is before determining its standard deviation.

How to Determine the Critical Path

The critical path is defined as the longest path traversing the network from the beginning to the end. In our example, the longest path is a-d-g-h. It takes longer to do the activities of that path than any of the others. Hence, the critical path is a-d-g-h. To determine the standard deviations of each of these activities, refer to Exhibit

6-9 and use the optimistic and pessimistic values of each of the activities. For activity a, the most optimistic time is six days, and the most pessimistic time is nine days. Using our formula for (, we can calculate the standard deviation for activity a.

$$\sigma = \frac{b - a}{6}$$

$$\sigma = \frac{9 - 6}{6}$$

$$\sigma = .5$$

In like manner, we calculate the standard deviations for activities d, g, and h to get the values .83, .33, and .33, respectively. The standard deviation for critical path, then, is:

$$SD_{\text{Critical Path}} = \sqrt{\sigma_1^2 + \sigma_2^2 + \sigma_3^2 \cdots \sigma_n^2}$$

$$= \sqrt{.25 + .69 + .11 + .11}$$

$$= \sqrt{1.16}$$

$$= 1.08 \text{ days}$$

The schedule length for our example project, for a 100 percent probability of completion, becomes:

$$T_e = 33.5 + 3 \times SD$$

$$= 33.5 + 3 \times 1.08 = 33.5 + 3.24$$

$$= 36.7 \text{ days}$$

Notice that in calculating standard deviation, we carried the decimals to two decimal places and the final schedule duration to one decimal place; all durations are estimates to begin with, so a rounding error is not of significant concern.

Slack or Float in a Project

One of the primary uses of a network analysis is to determine how much slack (or float; generally the terms are used interchangeably) is available in the project. *Slack* refers to the amount of extra time available between the end of one activity and the beginning of the succeeding one(s). It is not the same as lead or lag time. Slack results because the activities on noncritical paths finish sooner than those on the critical path, and therefore there is some extra time available before a succeeding activity must begin. *Lead* or *lag time*, on the other hand, is time built into the schedule to control the start and end times of activities.

Slack is important to the project manager because it allows leeway in starting times of certain activities so that the use of resources can be optimized. That is, if there are fewer personnel available to work on the project than are needed, then it may be possible to do the job anyway if some of the activities can be delayed, so that the total number of people needed is equal to or below the number available. This is called *resource leveling*. This schedule optimization can be accomplished only if there is some slack available in the project. We determine the amount of slack in a project by calculating the early start, early finish, late start, and late finish of each project. We already calculated the early finish (EF) for each of the activities in the example in Exhibit 6-10 when we calculated the EOT. The EF or EOT of the longest path will determine the schedule duration. Using the same example, Exhibit 6-10, let us calculate the other three values.

Calculating Early Start/Early Finish

The early start (ES) and early finish (EF) values are determined by starting from the first node. We have already determined these values, and they are shown in Exhibit 6-11. The early start for activity a is 0. Starting at 0, the earliest that an activity can end is 7.5 days, since it takes 7.5 days to accomplish the activity. The earliest that activities b, c, and d can start is 7.5 days. Notice that the ES of succeeding activities will be the EF of the previous activity, except where several activities feed into the same node, as into node 6. In

Exhibit 6-11. Early start and early finish times.

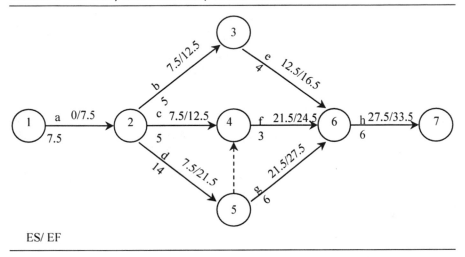

ES/ EF

this case, the ES for activity h will be the *larger* of the EF numbers feeding into the node.

Calculating Late Start/Late Finish

Calculating the late start (LS) and late finish (LF) numbers is done in the reverse order—that is, from the end of the network to the beginning. This occurs because we start with the schedule duration, found by determining the EF of the critical path, and work backward. Exhibit 6-12 shows the completed network analysis with all the times filled in. Note that the latest the project can finish is 33.5 days (we can use the estimated time, T_e, for this part of the analysis because the relative activity durations will yield the correct slack in the activity). The latest activity h can finish, then, is 33.5 days. The latest activity h can start is 27.5 days, since it takes six days to accomplish the activity. The latest that activities e, f, and g can finish will have to be the LS time of activity h since they each have to be finished in time for h to start. This process is continued backward through the network until the beginning is reached.

Notice what happens at node 2. We have a decision to make about which is the correct LF number for activity a, since we have three choices coming into node 2. This time, the correct number is

Exhibit 6-12. Early start, early finish, late start, and late finish times.

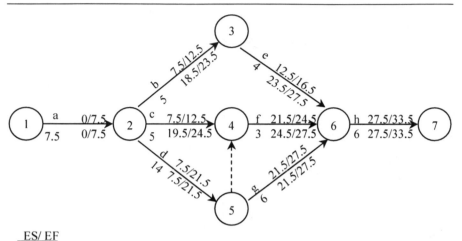

ES/ EF
LS/LF

the smaller of the choices. (Going forward through the network from beginning to end, the early finish is the larger number when there are several choices entering a single node; going backward through the network from the end to the beginning, the late start is the smaller number when there are several choices exiting for a single node.)

Slack in an activity is calculated by subtracting its early finish from the late finish or the early start from the late start of the activity. For instance, looking at Exhibit 6-12, the slack in activity b is 11 days. We can find the slack in the other activities in the same manner, that is, subtracting EF from LF. But notice that activities a, d, g, and h have zero slack. This is a second important characteristic of the critical path; the first characteristic is that the critical path is the longest path in the network, and the second is that the activities on the critical path have minimum or no slack (usually the slack on a critical path is zero). The zero slack is the reason that the critical path is called "critical." With zero slack available, any delay in any of the activities on the critical path will cause the project to miss its scheduled finish time. In essence, then, the project manager's focus is on managing the critical path activities.

Perhaps a few words to clarify critical activity or task are in order. In discussions about critical tasks, people who are new to the concept invariably assume that to have a critical task automatically means that there are also noncritical, in the sense of unimportant or less important, tasks. *There are no unimportant tasks; all tasks are critical in the sense that they are necessary for the completion of the project.* However, that is not the way we are using the terms *critical task* and *critical path.* By critical task I mean that it is a task that has minimal or zero slack and is on the path that defines the schedule. Hence, the task is critical because it directly affects the schedule if there is any delay in it.

Using the Precedence Diagramming Method

The PDM is the preferred network analysis method because it follows a logic diagram that is easier to visualize and construct, and it avoids the need for dummy activities. Project management software programs base their network analyses on the PDM because the dummy activities of the PERT method are not easy to model.

The analysis of the PDM is the same as in PERT once the duration estimates are known. That is, early and late start, early and late finish, schedule length, and the critical path are determined the same way in both methods. The difference is that in the PDM there are no dummy activities, and the activity information is presented on the nodes. To illustrate this difference, Exhibit 6-13 is the PDM view of the previous PERT analysis shown in Exhibit 6-12, the generic project example.

One final point needs to be made about PDM. Occasionally, you will not have an accurate duration estimate for one or more of the tasks in a project. You simply use the PERT method to determine the duration estimates for these tasks, and remember to apply a standard deviation for your estimate.

The Critical Path Method

The CPM is very similar to PERT, except that the duration times are not statistically determined. That means that the duration times for the activities of a project are known with a high degree

Exhibit 6-13. PDM view of the specific project.

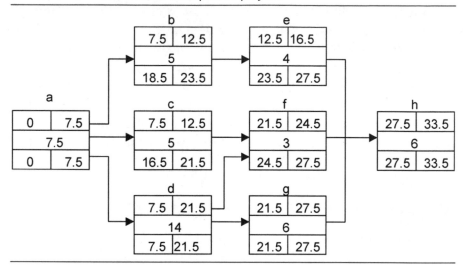

of accuracy, usually because of past experience and historical data on similar projects. The CPM method is used almost exclusively by the construction industry, and often by other industries as long as the project is straightforward and durations can be estimated with a high degree of accuracy. In the case of the CPM method, only one time is used for each estimated duration.

The CPM is an AOA type of network, so it looks exactly like the PERT network, and the analysis process is exactly the same. The major use of the CPM, though, is as a cost-estimating tool. The CPM is used to *crash the schedule,* which is a way of compressing the schedule. The reason this becomes a cost-estimating tool is that compressing the schedule usually requires adding resources, which adds costs to the project. Additional costs can be acceptable in a project provided that the benefits of crashing the schedule offset these costs. At some point, the costs become prohibitive, and crashing the schedule is no longer a viable option.

Crashing the schedule is accomplished by examining the activities on the critical path to determine if any of them can be shortened, either by increasing the resources or by doing some of the activity's subtasks in parallel. The process is to reduce one or more of the activities on the critical path by one time unit. For instance, if the duration units are days, then the critical path should be reduced by one day and the impact assessed. This process should continue until the desired result is achieved, a point is reached beyond which the costs are unacceptable, or the critical path is reduced to a point beyond which a new critical path is created.

Clearly, it is of no benefit to add resources to activities that are not on the critical path, because to do so would be adding costs with no attendant benefits in the schedule.

Summary

One major tool for the project manager is the network analysis. The three most common network analysis tools are the PERT, CPM, and PDM. The PERT is the only network tool that explicitly accounts for risk in schedule estimating. One of the disadvantages of both the PERT and the CPM is that there can be a potential for a dummy activity. Although the dummy is not hard to account for, it is an additional constraint that is not required in the PDM. Finally, one of the major advantages of the PDM is that alternative sequencing between activities is possible as well as the use of lead and lag times. Neither the PERT nor the CPM allows anything but finish-to-start sequencing in the activity relationships, and lead and lag times cannot be shown discretely in these methods. Lead and lag can be accommodated by PERT and CPM, but only by adding them to the individual task durations. Of course, doing so complicates project progress tracking.

CHAPTER 7

Earned Value

> Given for one instant an intelligence . . . if . . . this
> intelligence were vast enough to submit these data to
> analysis . . . to it nothing would be uncertain, and the future
> as the past would be present to its eyes."
>
> —PIERRE SIMON DE LAPLACE
> *Oeuvres*, vol. VII, "Théorie Analytique des Probabilités"

Prior to the 1960s, tracking project progress essentially consisted of monitoring the actual costs against the budget and the actual schedule against the estimate, but no method was available that assessed the combined impacts of costs and schedule. Nor were there any standards for analyzing and reporting these data. This problem came to a head in the Department of Defense because of the size and complexity of its projects. The problem was exacerbated by having multiple contractors working on the same project and all having their own tracking and reporting systems.

In the 1960s, with the U.S. Air Force taking the lead, the DOD set about to develop a DOD instruction, identified in governmental jargon as a DODI, that would provide guidance to contractors for:

- Developing work breakdown structures
- Developing certain key planning elements such as baselines
- Defining cost allocations and procedures for collecting and reporting cost data

- Analyzing budget and schedule variances and predicting future project costs
- Preparing performance reports

The first instruction, DODI 7000.2, was implemented in 1967. It took some time before DOD contractors fully embraced DODI 7000.2 because it required some radical changes in the accounting systems. The DOD allowed a period of transition but made it clear that to be awarded a DOD contract, the contractor had to abide by the requirements of DODI 7000.2. By the early 1970s, all DOD contractors had fully implemented the procedures required by the instruction.

The DODI 7000.2 has remained essentially unchanged since it was first written. It was superseded by DODI 5000.2 in 1991, with the primary change being a supplemental user guide, but with little else changing. This instruction is also known as the cost/schedule control system criteria (C/SCSC).

One of the most beneficial components of the C/SCSC is the method of project progress analysis known as earned value. This method was exclusively used by the DOD and its contractors until the late 1980s or early 1990s, when the private sector began to adopt it as the analysis of the tool of choice. The method can be used on both small and large projects and is independent of the type of contract executing the project.

The Earned Value Concept

The concept of earned value is sometimes difficult to grasp, although not because the concept or the procedure is difficult. (On the contrary, the procedure is very straightforward.) The problem is basically twofold: Earned value has a language of its own, and schedule is measured in terms of dollars instead of time. Since measuring schedule in this fashion goes against intuition and experience, some people focus on the language rather than on the concepts of earned value. The result is that learning the earned value analysis technique is harder than it should be.

The key to understanding earned value is in understanding the following three terms:

1. Planned estimate of work scheduled (PV)
2. Actual cost of work performed (AC)
3. Amount of money budgeted for the work that is actually performed or the earned value of work performed (EV)

Planned Estimate of Work Scheduled

The PV is the project budget, or what is expected to be spent to accomplish the project objectives. The meaning of this term is not very different from our usual understanding. The project manager gets the components of PV from the work breakdown structure and constructs a cumulative, time-phased graph showing the anticipated budget from the start of the project to the end. This budget line is the standard against which the project expenditures are measured, bringing us to the next definition of interest, AC.

Actual Cost of Work Performed

AC too is a very familiar concept. The AC is what it costs to do the project. In other words, AC is what is actually spent in performing the tasks of the project.

Prior to the development of the earned value analysis technique, the PV and the AC were used to analyze project progress by a comparison of budget and actual expenditures. The problem is that this type of analysis does not account for the impact of schedule variances, at least not in any way that is obvious or interpretable. For instance, at the end of month six, the AC might be higher than the budget for that period. On the surface, this would indicate that the project was overspending its budget. It might be, however, that one or more of the tasks were started and completed earlier than planned so that more money was expended but more work was accomplished. This problem led to our next term, the EV, or earned value.

Earned Value of Work Performed

The EV element of the earned value analysis is the term and concept that is different from how we usually view schedule tracking. The C/SCSC developed a method for tracking schedules in terms of dollars earned for the actual amount of work accomplished, or EV. People new to the concept of earned value often have trouble separating this term from the actual cost of the task or project, but there is a significant difference between the AC and the EV. The AC represents the amount of money *actually spent* on the work completed; the EV is the amount of money *budgeted* for the work that has been completed.

To explain the concept of EV, we will start with the *fifty-fifty rule*, a widely accepted method for determining how much work has been completed at any analysis point in the project. The rule was adopted as a way to estimate how much work has been completed on a task or project. Suppose there is a contract to manufacture 100 desk chairs, and they are to be delivered in four weeks. If the project manager's schedule is to produce twenty-five chairs per week, then it is not difficult to determine whether the project is ahead or behind schedule when the newly manufactured chairs are counted at the end of every week. If, however, the project is to develop software or is some type of services effort, then determining what percentage of the work has been accomplished at random times in the project's life is difficult, if not impossible. Hence the development of the fifty-fifty rule.

The fifty-fifty rule assumes that when a task begins, it is 50 percent complete; when the task is completed, it is 100 percent complete. The reason for this assumption is to provide a consistent means of estimating how much of the planned work was accomplished—that is, EV—at any point in the task. This method is so widely accepted that a contractor has to justify using any other method before a customer will approve it. But there is an obvious problem with the fifty-fifty rule. If a project's status is taken immediately after a task begins, then the project manager can take credit for finishing 50 percent of the task's work virtually before it even begins. And if the status is taken near the end of the task, the project may actually be 90 percent complete but can take credit for only half of it. Exhibit 7-1 more clearly depicts the fifty-fifty rule.

There are four tasks shown in Exhibit 7-1, and, for the sake of simplicity, we have estimated the budget of each to be $1,000. From the exhibit, we can see that Task 1 began on time and finished on time. Since we budgeted Task 1 to cost $1,000, we can take full credit for it. Task 2 started on time and was completed early. Therefore, we can take full credit, or $1,000, for this task. Task 3 was supposed to have started but has not, so we get no credit for the task. Task 4 started late but hasn't been completed, so we get 50 percent credit, or $500, for starting the task. To summarize, the EV for these tasks is:

Exhibit 7-1. Determining EV by the fifty-fifty rule.

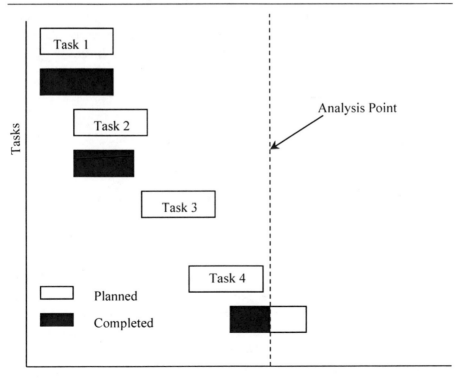

Task 1	$1,000
Task 2	1,000
Task 3	0
Task 4	500
	$2,500

The EV for these four tasks is $2,500. We also know what the planned estimate of work scheduled (PV) is. Since we budgeted $1,000 for each of the tasks, the PV is $4,000. (If the dotted line in Exhibit 7-1 had cut through any of the planned boxes, we would use the fifty-fifty rule to determine the percentage to apply to determine PV as we did for the EV.)

Notice that I have said nothing about the actual cost of the work to this point. Suppose the expenditure for Task 1 was $1,000—right on budget. But Task 2 didn't take as long as we had anticipated, so we spent less, say, $800. Task 3 hasn't started yet, so nothing has been spent on it. Now suppose we have spent $600 to date on Task 4. Summarizing our actual costs, we have:

Task 1	$1,000
Task 2	800
Task 3	0
Task 4	600
	$2,400

Therefore, the PV = $4,000, AC = $2,400, and EV = $2,500 for this particular time in the project's life cycle. So what do these numbers tell us?

If EV is the amount we have earned and AC is the amount we have spent, it is clear that we are spending at a slower rate than we are earning (EV − AC = 2,500 − 2,400 = 100). Hence, the project is under budget by $100. And, if EV is the amount we have earned and PV is the amount scheduled to spend, then clearly we are behind schedule (EV − PV = 2,500 − 4000 = −1,500). Remember that we have converted schedule to a dollar basis. Hence, we interpret the negative result as showing that we have not earned as much as we had scheduled to have earned.

Because some organizations, or some customers, are more conservative than the fifty-fifty rule will accommodate, other methods for estimating percent of work completion are used. For instance, some organizations use a 20 percent credit for beginning a task and 80 percent at completion; others are more conservative and give no credit for starting a task and 100 percent credit only when it is completed. Even so, the fifty-fifty rule is by far the most common method for estimating percentage of task completion when it is not possible to determine the actual amount of work completed.

Evaluating Project Status

The rationale of earned value can be represented by some easy-to-remember formulas. Comparing the amount earned in a project to the amount spent is what we call *cost variance* and is represented by the formula:

$$CV = EV - AC$$

The comparison of EV to PV is called *schedule variance,* and it is represented by the formula:

$$SV = EV - PV$$

Note that in both these equations, the first term on the right side of the equation is EV. EV is the key component for both these equations because this is the earned value term, or the amount earned toward completion of the project.

An example will better demonstrate the use of these formulas. Suppose you assess project progress at the planned 60 percent completion point for a $20,000 project, and you find that you have completed only 50 percent of the work. At this point, the PV is $12,000 (.60 × $20,000 = $12,000), and the EV is $10,000 (.50 × $20,000 = $10,000). Suppose further that the actual money expended for the work accomplished is $8,000. The cost variance is:

$$CV = EV - AC$$

or

$$CV = 10{,}000 - 8{,}000$$

and

$$CV = \$2{,}000$$

A positive CV indicates that the project is under budget, and a negative CV indicates that the project is over budget. Of course, if the CV equals zero, then the project is on budget.

The SV for this task is:

$$SV = EV - PV$$

or

$$SV = 10{,}000 - 12{,}000$$

and

$$SV = -\$2{,}000$$

A negative SV indicates that the project is behind schedule; a positive SV indicates that the project is ahead of schedule; and a SV equal to zero means that the project is exactly on schedule.

There are several other mathematical terms and equations important to the earned value techniques. These are the cost performance index (CPI), the schedule performance index (SPI), the budget at completion (BAC), the estimate to complete (ETC), and the estimate at completion (EAC). Each of these terms and their equations are discussed in detail below.

Performance Indexes

It is often more meaningful to have some percentage measurement or index of how the project is doing. The two most often used indexes are the cost performance index (CPI) and the schedule performance index (SPI). The same terms are used for each of these as were used to determine CV and SV, respectively, except that instead of subtracting the terms, we divide them. Hence, we have:

$$CPI = \frac{EV}{AC}$$

and

$$SPI = \frac{EV}{PV}$$

David Frame refers to the CPI as the "burn rate" or the rate at which we are spending money, and this is a very good way to look at it.[1] Another way of looking at CPI and SPI is as efficiency rates. For example, using our previous example, where EV = 10,000 and AC = 8,000, the CPI is:

$$CPI = \frac{10,000}{8,000} = 1.25$$

This means that we are making money faster than we are "burning" it. Looking at it as an efficiency rate, we are making twenty-five cents for every dollar we are spending.

The schedule performance index (SPI) can be analyzed in the same way. Again, using our previous example, the EV = 10,000 and PV = 12,000. The SPI becomes:

$$SPI = \frac{10,000}{12,000} = 0.83 \text{ (rounded to the nearest 100th)}$$

Hence, we have accomplished only a little over three-fourths of the work that was scheduled, or the job is only 83 percent complete.

Estimate at Completion and Estimate to Complete

Two important terms—estimate at completion (EAC) and estimate to complete (ETC)—sound very similar but yield different, although related, information.

Estimate at completion is the estimated final cost of the project. A new EAC is determined as the project progresses and more information is available to the project manager relative to how realistic the original budget and schedule estimates were. Also, unexpected events occur that positively or negatively impact the project, thus making the original estimated total cost of the project wrong.

The *estimate to complete* is the estimate of the amount of money that is required to finish the project from the point a progress analysis is made to the end of the project. In short, EAC is the difference between the new estimate at completion and the amount of money actually spent to date.

Estimate at Completion

It is important to keep a running tab of the total cost of the project. At the beginning of the project, the project team will have determined a budget, called the budget at completion (BAC). Depending upon how the project is progressing, the original budget might not hold up. Therefore, every time the project manager takes a snapshot in time to determine how the project is doing, one of the key elements of the analysis is a new estimate at completion (EAC), calculated as:

$$EAC = \frac{BAC}{CPI}$$

Suppose that the total project's budget at completion was \$20,000. With our CPI of 1.25, the new estimate at completion, at our current rate of performance, would be:

$$EAC = \frac{20,000}{1.25}$$

$$= \$16,000$$

Hence, at this point in the project's life cycle, we are doing better than our original total budget estimate. At the current rate, the project will only cost $16,000, $4,000 less than our original estimate.

Estimate to Complete

Once the new estimate at completion is determined, the final key element of the earned value analysis can be calculated: the estimate to complete or the amount of money needed to complete the project from this point.

The ETC is calculated by:

$$ETC = EAC - AC$$

In the example, the ETC is $16,000 and the AC is $8,000. Therefore, our new estimate to complete the project is:

$$ETC = 16,000 - 8,000$$
$$= \$8,000$$

Exhibit 7-2 explains the various elements of the earned value analysis and shows the relationship of each. Exhibit 7-3 summarizes the key earned value formulas discussed in this chapter.

The Critical Ratio

The critical ratio (CR) is another useful indicator of a project's health, and a quick check of how the project is doing overall. The CR is referred to as the cost-schedule index.

The CR is the product of CPI and SPI, or $CR = CPI \times SPI$. For the previous example, $CR = 1.25 \times 0.83 = 1.04$, which indicates the project is on track—that is, it is behind schedule but below budget.

A CR of 1.00 indicates that overall, the project performance is on target, which may result from both CPI and SPI being on or near target. But if one of the indexes suggests poor performance, the other suggests good performance. Hence an opportunity for

Exhibit 7-2. Elements of earned-value analysis.

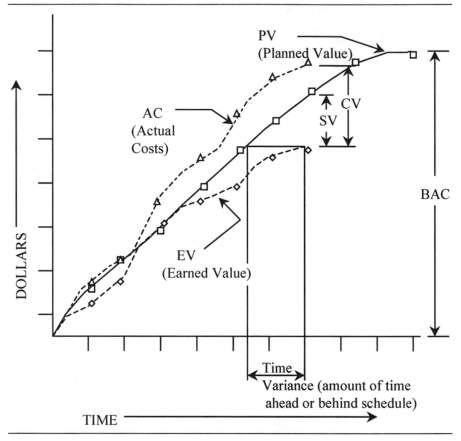

some trade-offs—for example, spending more to improve the schedule.

A CR of less than 1.0 indicates poor performance, which generally results when both the CPI and the SPI are below target (but not necessarily; one may indicate a good performance; the other's performance is sufficiently poor that overall, the project is in trouble).

A CR greater than 1.0 is a measure of excellent performance and usually results when both the CPI and the SPI show good performance. Again, one of these indexes can be indicating poor performance while the other shows outstanding performance. In this case, the project manager has a large trade-off opportunity. In short, the CR is an excellent tool for the project manager to assess

Exhibit 7-3. Summary of earned value formulas.

FORMULA	CALCULATES	NOTES
CV = EV − AC	Cost Variance	Positive value indicates under budget; negative, over budget
SV = EV − PV	Schedule Variance	Positive value indicates ahead of schedule; negative, behind schedule
CPI = EV/AC	Cost Performance Index	Value greater than one (1) indicates under budget; less than one, over budget
SPI = EV/PV	Schedule Performance Index	Value greater than one (1) indicates ahead of schedule; less than one, over schedule
EAC = BAC/CPI	Estimate at Completion	New estimate of the cost of the project
ETC = EAC − AC	Estimate to Complete	Amount of money needed to complete the project from the analysis point

the project's health quickly and determine visually where to make trade-offs to bring the project back to target. Exhibit 7-4 shows a CR graph, while Exhibit 7-5 provides some general guidance about the overall health of the project and indicates to the project manager when to make trade-offs to correct the project's progress.

Summary

The earned value analysis technique was developed by the Department of Defense when it became obvious that a standard method

Exhibit 7-4. Critical ratio graph.

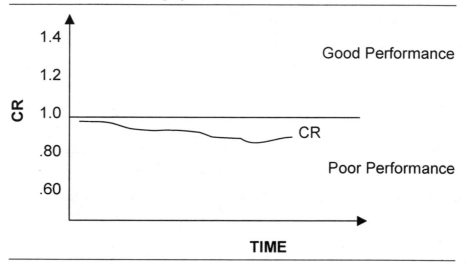

Exhibit 7-5. Project target performance chart.

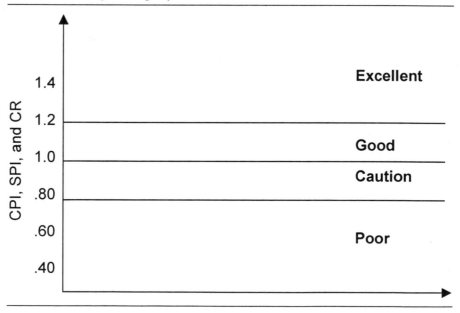

was needed to track, analyze, and report project progress. The result was a DOD instruction that defines cost and schedule criteria, known as the cost/schedule control system criteria. One of the most important tools to come out of the DOD is the earned value technique, which explicitly accounts for schedule impacts by identifying a way to associate schedule with percentage of work completed, or "earned."

Although the earned value method was developed by the DOD to be used by defense contractors, the method has been discovered by the private sector as well. It is now widely used for tracking and analyzing project progress not only because it is the most accurate method developed to date but also because it can be used very effectively with both small and large projects. In addition, the earned value concept is contract-independent. That is, regardless of whether the contract is a fixed-fee or cost-plus type of contract, an earned value analysis is equally usable and effective.

PART TWO

Managing a Project

Introduction to Part Two

Part One discussed the various human and technical skills and tools needed for project management. Part Two discusses where and when to apply this knowledge.

A project has a life cycle with several phases, much the same as a human: It starts slowly in the concept and development phases, builds during development to a peak in the implementation phases, and then begins a steady decline until termination. It is often difficult to differentiate between a project's life cycle phases because some overlapping of activities or tasks is inevitable. Even so, it is useful to think in terms of discrete life cycle phases because that facilitates identification of typical project management activities and the associated skills and tools to accomplish them. Exhibit PII-1 depicts a typical project having four phases: concept, development, implementation, and termination. The usual activities for each phase are listed along with the tools most often used. Note that the human characteristics and skills of communication, negotiation, leadership, team building, and coping extend across every phase.

The Part Two chapters follow the sequence of a project's life so that the process of managing a project will be clearly defined. This approach provides a good understanding of what activities are likely to occur in each phase, what the project manager and his or her team's action should be, and which tools and skills to use in formulating a response to the activity.

Exhibit PII–1. The life cycle of a project, project activities, and required project management skills.

THE PROJECT LIFE CYCLE

Concept	Development	Implementation	Termination
Activities	**Activities**	**Activities**	**Activities**
•Gather data. •Identify requirements. •Develop alternatives. •Estimate resources. •Develop charter.	•Appoint core team. •Write project plan. •Develop scope baseline. •Obtain approval to proceed. •Develop network analysis. •Kick off project.	•Set up project organization. •Establish detailed requirements. •Set up and execute work packages. •Direct, monitor, and control project.	•Review and accept project. •Sign off and transfer responsibility. •Document and evaluate results. •Release and redirect resources.
Tools	**Tools**	**Tools**	**Tools**
•Contract, specifications statement of work (SOW) •Work Breakdown Structure (WBS)	•Project management plan •WBS •Gantt chart •PERT/PDM •Risk management plan	•WBS •Gantt chart •Earned value •Risk management plan •Reports	•Management plan •WBS •Technical/financial audits •Reports

Human Skills Required

Communications
Negotiation
Leadership
Team-Building
Coping

CHAPTER 8

Project and Project Manager Selection

It is not enough to appoint project managers,
hand them the ball, and tell them to run with it.

—LINN C. STUCKENBRUCK
then-professor, University of Southern California

All projects have a genesis, a starting point. There is a process in every organization that gets projects on the active list; that is, determines which of several opportunities the organization will fund or support through the competition cycle. How do these projects get started? What are the criteria for choosing one project over another, for deciding which project offers a greater opportunity for the organization than another does? After the project is chosen, how is the project manager selected? This chapter looks at these questions and provides a clear understanding of how these processes work.

Methods for Choosing the Project and Getting Organizational Commitment

In most companies, it is very likely that the project managers are not involved in the project selection process at all. The new business and marketing staff typically identify potential projects and then "sell" the senior management on the importance of the individual project to the organization. It is only after the project makes the list of business opportunities that a project manager is selected and assigned to the project. There are exceptions, however; the project manager might find him- or herself in the position of participating in the selection process. Not only that, but many companies do not have any identifiable process for selecting projects; they simply go after any contract that seems to have some similarity to previous work done. For both reasons, a clear understanding of how projects are started and selected and prioritized is important.

Selection Model Criteria

Basically, there are two types of selection models: nonnumeric and numeric. Numeric models are often further categorized into either profit or profitability and scoring or ranking. Organizations that use models to help in the selection and prioritization of projects often use a combination of these types, but the use of models runs the gambit from "gut feel" to highly sophisticated mathematical simulations.

Models, whether nonnumeric or numeric, should have certain characteristics. The following six basic criteria define good models:

1. *Realism.* There are any number of projects that could benefit the organization. However, if a model, or user of the model, does not take into consideration the technical and cost risks, capital outlay for facilities, and people resources, then any project selected with the model would not reflect a realistic choice.

2. *Capability.* Projects tend to be complex, particularly if they involve high technology or a large engineering or construction effort. Therefore, the model used has to be sophisticated enough to handle multiple-task, multiyear simulations, and it should be able to make comparisons between different projects based on the constraints placed by decision makers. Otherwise, the project cannot be accurately simulated.

3. *Flexibility.* Flexibility in a model may be its most important characteristic. Given the complexity of most projects, numerous iterations and what-if scenarios are needed before a prediction of a project's worth to the organization can be made. Furthermore, the project will undoubtedly undergo numerous changes during its lifetime, requiring new evaluations of the project and project status against the organization's strategic business plan. The model must be flexible enough to handle these evaluations.

4. *Ease of Use.* A major disadvantage of many numeric models is that they require specialized knowledge or sophisticated computer programming to use them. Consequently, many otherwise accurate models are not used. Any model should be simple enough to use that any participants in the process can quickly and effectively input required data and extract usable information. Most nonnumeric, and in many cases numeric, models can be set up to use standard software. For instance, most models can be programmed into any of the good spreadsheets such as Excel or Quattro-Pro, or project selection software can be purchased that is compatible with, or is a plug-in to, the spreadsheet.

5. *Cost-Effectiveness.* Most common selection models are not expensive. In fact, the nonnumeric models themselves do not cost anything. However, they can be expensive in terms of labor hours needed to employ them or to program them for general use. Numeric models, particularly highly sophisticated simulations, can require initial capital outlay for the software or the cost of the labor to program them. Regardless, the model should never be more expensive than the projects they are analyzing. They should be as economical as possible and still be as sophisticated as needed to do the required analysis.

6. *Ease of Computerization.* Powerful data manipulation packages are readily available on personal computers today, and these common databases, such as d-Base, Access, and Fox Pro, are of benefit in structuring selection models. Even if the model itself is difficult to use, it can usually be programmed in such a way that the user has only to input the data, and the program will make the requisite calculations and provide a translatable readout.

Nonnumeric Selection Models

Groups are most comfortable with brainstorming techniques for prioritizing projects or any tasks. So tools that enable this process are of particular value. Also, many people are "math challenged" and are not comfortable with processes that require analyzing numeric methods. Fortunately, several very good nonnumeric models can facilitate brainstorming without the need for numeric analysis. Here are a few of the best methods.

Q-Sort Model

An excellent method for prioritizing projects within an organization is called the Q-Sort method.[1] This method is by far one of the most straightforward nonnumeric methods and can be used for anything that involves prioritization of events or projects or for identification of problems.

In general, the Q-Sort method follows this initial procedure:

1. Write the potential projects on 5- by 7-inch index cards, one project per card.

2. Divide the stack of cards into three stacks: good, fair, and poor. Good, fair, and poor are subjective measures of the relative worth to the organization of the projects being considered. So it is important that participants be knowledgeable about the company's business so that project merits can be assessed and ranked. The number of cards per stack does not have to be equal, but none of the stacks should have more than eight cards.

3. If any of the stacks have more than eight cards, the cards are further divided into better and worse groups. For example, if the "poor" stack has more than eight cards, it can be subdivided into better-than-average poor, poor, and worse-than-average poor.

4. Continue this process until none of the stacks contain more than eight cards.

Once this initial sorting is completed, each of the stacks is then subjected to the Q-Sort process. The Q-Sort process can be done by one person who has the responsibility for the prioritization, but it is better if done by a committee. If the process is done by a committee, each member is given a copy of a stack of cards. Then each participant begins the Q-Sort process, which consists of the following five steps:

1. Each participant receives a stack of cards containing the project name and any required descriptive information.

2. Each participant then divides her stack into two stacks: one being high-priority-level and the other being low-priority-level. The delineation between high and low levels can be determined by some sort of weighting or measuring criteria or simply based on the participant's best judgment. Remember that these two stacks do not have to be equal in size.

3. Each participant builds a third stack by reexamining both the high- and low-priority stacks for borderline or questionable entries. This third stack of cards will become the medium-priority level.

4. Each participant will examine both the high- and low-priority stacks to form two additional stacks of very-high-priority and very-low-priority stacks. At this point, each participant should have five stacks representing very high, high, medium, low, and very low priorities.

5. Each of the participants may readjust any or all of the stacks as she sees fit.

A facilitator gathers all the stacks and summarizes and combines them until a consensus is reached. A graphical depiction of the Q-Sort method is shown in Exhibit 8-1.

The Peer Review Method

The peer review method, or a variation of it, is one of the most widely used methods for choosing projects. This is the method most often used by government agencies such as the National In-

Exhibit 8-1. The Q-Sort process.

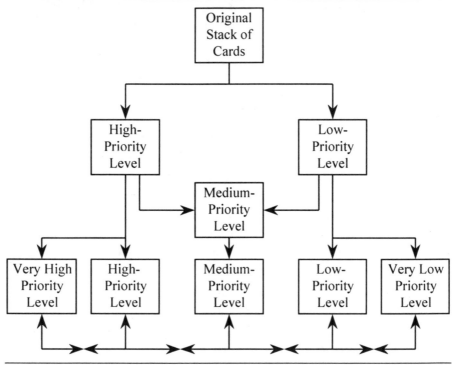

Source: Adapted from A. F. Helin and W. E. Souder, "Experimental Test of a Q-Sort Procedure for Prioritizing R&D Projects," *IEEE Transactions on Engineering Management* (November 1974).

stitutes of Health and the National Science Foundation to select projects. It is also often used in other research-and-development laboratories for prioritizing or selecting projects.

Typically, the peer review method consists of three to five competent people from outside the organization who are chosen to assess the proposal. Each of these independent evaluators is given a copy of the proposal and asked to rate it against some predetermined criteria. The evaluations are tabulated and compared. Naturally, if a project is rated low by all or a consensus of the group, it will not be funded. Likewise, a project with mixed ratings probably won't be funded either. Only those projects receiving high ratings from a strong majority of the group will even be considered.

Closer to home, a variation of the peer review is used in many companies to decide whether to pursue a proposal. This method is especially popular in companies that rely heavily on Department of Defense contracts because it is a fast and easy way to determine whether the company has the technical and resource capability to write a credible proposal and perform the work if they win the contract. In this version, copies of the solicitation, usually in the form of a request for proposal (RFP), are sent to key people who have recognized expertise in the RFP requirements or who have experience with the customer and the likely competitors for the business. The facilitator in this process is usually a key marketing or new business development person who provides the RFP and whatever additional marketing intelligence is available. Often, one or more of the evaluators will express an interest in having the lead for the project should a decision be made to pursue it. Naturally, unless there is strong support or interest in the project, it is not pursued. If there is strong interest in the project, the marketing or new-business-development person and someone from the functional area most likely to be responsible for the contracted work will develop a proposal strategy and a strategy for getting the project on the organization's pursuit list.

Murder Board

The murder board is used in virtually every company in some form for project selection but is especially popular, and useful, in companies dependent on competitive bids for their business. (Its name stems from the fact that members of the board try to find a reason not to pursue a project. In other words, they "kill" it.) The murder board is generally the highest-level board or group that examines potential and ongoing proposal efforts to determine whether a project should be pursued or continued. Furthermore, it is a fast and easy method for selecting and discarding projects.

The senior managers of the organization comprise the murder board. Usually that means that each of the vice presidents is automatically a member of the board. The board is usually chaired by the vice president of new business or of marketing, depending on how the organization is structured.

Basically, the murder board meets on a regular basis, usually once a month, to hear briefings on key projects. The key project representative, proposal manager, marketing lead, or project manager, as appropriate, briefs the project to the board. The murder board's function is to disqualify or "kill" the project if they can. That is, they attempt to find reasons that the organization should not pursue or continue the project. Consequently, the briefer(s) have to be prepared to counter any argument that is made for eliminating the project. If they are successful in defending their project to the murder board, then it is allowed to continue to whatever the next phase is.

In spite of the ease and usefulness of the murder board, there are three major problems with this approach.

1. It is a negative approach, which impedes brainstorming the potential project for ways to strengthen it and make it viable.

2. It often fosters a competitive environment among the board members to see who can "destroy" the briefer first. The result is that everyone hates going before the murder board and do so reluctantly. The briefings are always designed to short-circuit the board's intent by playing to the biases of the board members and avoiding any subject that could lead to project disqualification. In short, since the briefer is penalized for identifying potential problem areas, he or she does not. Hence, decisions about the projects are based on incomplete data. If the murder board operated in a collaborative fashion, where risks and concerns are discussed and dealt with, then some projects that might otherwise be disqualified become viable. Furthermore, there would be fewer surprises during the life of those projects that are qualified on inaccurate data.

3. Many people are not good at briefing a hostile audience. As a result, many projects are disqualified because the briefer could not perform well enough, not because the project lacked merit.

Poor Man's Hierarchy

In his book on project management, J. Davidson Frame (the academic dean at the University of Management and Technology in Rosslyn, Virginia) describes a pared-down treatment of a decision-making tool called the analytical hierarchy process (AHP).[2] Frame developed the method as an introduction to the AHP, but the method is a good decision-making tool in its own right. He calls this tool the *poor man's hierarchy*.

The method is straightforward and easy to use. It requires only that some baseline criteria be established against which the project will be measured. A square grid is constructed, and the criteria are listed along the left-hand side and across the top of the grid. Then each individual criterion on the left-hand side of the grid is assessed in turn against all the remaining criteria across the top of the grid. As each criterion down the left side is assessed, it is assigned a 1 if it is more important than the criterion across the top and a 0 if it is less important. Naturally, the criteria are not assessed against themselves in the process, so the diagonal of the grid is left blank. When all the criteria are assessed in this fashion, the numbers are totaled for each. The criteria are sorted by total rating, largest number first, to rank them in order. This method can be used to assess the criteria of an individual project, as in Exhibit 8-2, or it can be used to prioritize projects within the organization.

Numeric Selection Models

Several numeric selection tools based on complex mathematical models are available. These methods are most often used in a research-and-development environment where significant risk and uncertainty exists. Since this book is more general in nature, I discuss only the more common selection models here.[3]

Payback Period

One of the most common selection tools is the *payback period*, defined as that period in a project's life cycle after which the cumulative annual cash inflow exceeds the expenditures for the project.

Exhibit 8-2. Example of poor man's hierarchy.

	Ada Programming	Cost	Portability	Maintainability	Reliability	Ease of Revision	Total Rating
Ada Programming		1	0	0	0	1	2
Cost	0		1	0	0	0	1
Portability	1	0		0	0	1	2
Maintainability	1	1	1		1	1	5
Reliability	1	1	1	0		1	4
Ease of Revision	0	1	0	0	0		1

Source: Adapted from J. Davidson Frame, *The New Project Management* (San Francisco: Jossey-Bass, 1994). Reprinted with permission. Copyright © 1994, Jossey-Bass, Inc., Publishers. All rights reserved.

The *payback point* is that point where the cumulative revenues exactly equal the expenditures. Usually, the expenditures are taken to be the initial investment.

Suppose an organization plans to install a new piece of equipment to make computer chips. The cost of the equipment is $200,000, and the expected annual revenue is $50,000. The payback period is calculated as follows:

$$\text{Payback Period} = \frac{200,000}{50,000}.$$

$$= 4 \text{ years}$$

Although this method is used often by senior managers and financial officers, it is a poor selection tool because it does not take into account the cost of money, that is, inflation. It assumes that revenues will continue beyond the payback period, and it does not account for risk. An early payback period implies that the risk is less than a later payback period. The fact is that risk is not explicitly considered at all unless a risk factor is included in the calculation of the annual revenues, and that is seldom done.

Average Rate of Return or Return on Investment

The average rate of return (ARR) is another favorite selection tool, but it suffers from the same disadvantages of the payback method: It does not account for the cost of money, does not consider future profits, and assumes there is less risk the larger the rate of return.

The primary reason for discussing the ARR method here is to point out a common mistake: Most people assume the ARR is just the inverse of the payback period. Notice, though, that the payback period definition includes annual revenues. The definition of ARR is the cost of initial investment divided by the annual expected profits.

Suppose in the example of the payback period that the expected annual profits are $20,000. Then the average rate of return is:

$$\text{ARR} = \frac{20,000}{200,000}$$

$$= .10 \text{ or } 10\%$$

If we use the simple inverse of the payback period as the ARR, then the ARR would be:

$$\text{ARR} = \frac{50,000}{200,000}$$

$$= .25 \text{ or } 25\%$$

Considering the shortcomings of this method relative to risks, it is easy to see how false expectations can be generated with the erroneous expectation of a 25 percent rate of return. The problem, of course, is that revenues include profit but other cash inflows as well, such as payment for work completed on a contract.

Neither the payback period nor the ARR method is recommended as a selection tool for the reasons stated. However, both are often used for this purpose principally because they are simple and fast. One advantage of these methods, other than their simplicity, is that they can be used to help plan organizational cash flow. They could also be used as a quick, approximate measure of merit or for measuring relative rankings of several projects. Otherwise they should be applied with great caution, and never as the only measure, if they are to be used as tools for project selection.

Benefit-to-Cost Ratio

Among the several variations of benefit-to-cost ratio methods, the most widely used one involves calculating the net present value (NPV) of costs and revenues. The NPV predicts the value of future worth in terms of today's dollars. In other words, it explicitly includes inflation as well as expected or desired profits.

Determining an accurate benefit-to-cost ratio can be difficult because items such as cost avoidance of labor, maintenance, efficiency of new equipment, and processes have to be quantified. Once that is done, the NPV method yields accurate estimates on which a reasoned decision can be made.

The formula for net present value is:

$$NPV = \sum_{t=0}^{n} \frac{F_t}{(1 + k)^t}$$

where:
   F_t = future cash flow at time t
   k = rate of return, which can have two components: estimated rate of inflation, i, and required or desired profit, p. Hence, k = i + p.
   Σ = the mathematical symbol meaning to sum the cash flow for any entry in the range of $t = 0$ through the last period, n.

As an example of the NPV method, suppose we have determined that a new management information system for the organization will require a $50,000 capital expense immediately and another $10,000 in six months. The benefit to the organization will be worth $10,000 at the six-month mark and $20,000 at six-month intervals until the end of the second year. The inflation rate is estimated to be 6 percent, and senior management would like to realize a 12 percent return or profit as a result of the new system. What is the benefit-to-cost ratio for this project?

A sketch of the project costs and revenues is shown in Exhibit 8-3. It is recommended that any analysis using NPV be laid out in this fashion because it helps to keep the time intervals and cash flow categories straight. You will see from the problem that determining the proper value of k is crucial since the magnitude of this term dramatically affects the outcome of the benefit-to-cost ratio analysis.

The NPV for the revenues (NPV_r) is:

$$NPV_r = \frac{10,000}{(1 + .09)^1} + \frac{20,000}{(1 + .09)^2} + \frac{20,000}{(1 + .09)^3} + \frac{20,000}{(1 + .09)^4}$$

Note that $k = i + p = .06 + .12 = .18$, but the time increments are six-month intervals. Therefore, the rate of return for each six months is .09.

Exhibit 8-3. Layout of cash flow estimates.

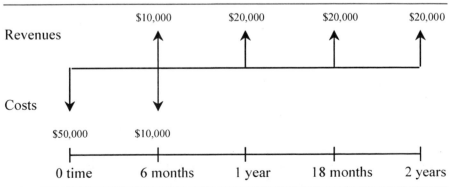

When we perform the operations of the equation above, NPV_r becomes:

$$NPV_r = \frac{10{,}000}{1.09} + \frac{20{,}000}{1.19} + \frac{20{,}000}{1.30} + \frac{20{,}000}{1.41}$$

or, $NPV_r = 9{,}174.31 + 16{,}806.72 + 15{,}384.62 + 14{,}184.40$

and $NPV_r = 55{,}550.05$

We now have to calculate the NPV for the costs of the project (NPV_c):

$$NPV_c = \frac{50{,}000}{(1 + .09)^0} + \frac{10{,}000}{(1 + .09)^1}$$

$$= \frac{50{,}000}{1} + \frac{10{,}000}{1.09}$$

$$= 50{,}000 + 9174.31$$

$$= 59{,}174.31$$

Note that in the first term in the first part of the equation, since the $50,000 cost was required immediately, then $t = 0$ and anything raised to the zero power equals 1. Hence, as you would expect, the $50,000 is not discounted because it is already in current dollars.

To calculate the benefit-to-cost ratio, we simply divide the NPV of the revenues by the NPV of the costs. Hence, for the example, the benefit-to-cost ratio (BCR) is:

$$BCR = \frac{NPV_r}{NPV_c}$$

$$= \frac{55{,}550.05}{59{,}174.31}$$

$$= .94$$

To realize a positive return on investment, the BCR has to be greater than one; to break even, the BCR has to be one; less than one indicates that costs outweigh the revenues.

The benefits of the example appear to outweigh the costs of the management information system at first glance, but when the future value of the cash flow is accounted for, the benefit-to-cost ratio for the first two years at least clearly shows that the organization cannot expect any positive return on the investment. However, if the benefits from the system continue beyond the second year, it is obvious that the payback period would occur shortly after the second year and the BCR will be greater than one. If the benefits are not expected to continue after the second year, then management would have to lower its expectations about the desired rate of profit they want as a result of the new system.

Process of Selecting a Project Manager

Once the project is selected, the real problem is choosing the right project manager to run it. The project manager is the key to a successful project. Choosing the wrong person can quickly turn what could have been a profitable endeavor into an economic and political disaster.

Well into the 1980s, project managers were chosen from those who had the most seniority or who had been a successful project engineer. It was almost universally accepted that project managers had to be engineers. It was rare that a project manager had any prior formal project management training; all project management training was done on the job. This type of experience and training is not all bad; working on a project is the best classroom there is. But there is more to running a project successfully than just understanding how to schedule work or prepare progress reports. The project manager needs a whole host of skills, as was treated in the discussion of project management skills in Chapter 1.

Organizations are now being more selective about whom they choose to put in the project management pool, and they are beginning to ensure that these people have the requisite skills, training, and experience. Just as being the top salesperson does not ensure that the person will be a good director of marketing, neither does being a good project engineer ensure that the person will succeed as a project manager. The basic skills needed by a successful project manager fall into four categories: personal characteristics, behavioral skills, general business skills, and technical skills.

Personal Characteristics

The most important personal characteristics needed by a successful project manager are:

- Flexible and adaptable
- Possessing and exhibiting initiative and leadership
- Confident and persuasive
- Possessing verbal fluency
- Able to balance technical and human components of a project
- Problem-solving and decision-making capability
- Good time manager

I would add one more: a sense of humor. Given that the work life of a project manager is a life of conflict, a sense of humor is critical for the manager's own well-being.

Behavioral Skills

Gone are the days when project managers could successfully complete a project through intimidation and a heavy-handed management style. The real key to success is through leadership, mentoring, coaching, and negotiation. The project manager must have a strong, active, and continuous interest in teaching, training, and developing subordinates. Without these skills, the project manager may succeed in the short term, but the long-term damage is irreparable. Strong interpersonal skills and the ability to listen actively and communicate are requirements if the project manager hopes to get unqualified support from the project team, the customer, and the rest of the organization.

General Business Skills

The project, large or small, is like a little company in which the project manager is the general manager. A general business education, formal or not, is crucial to guiding the project through its life cycle in consonance with the strategic goals of the parent organization. Most project managers are given the profit-and-loss responsibility of the project and of necessity have to understand what that means and how to manage within the bounds of solid business practices. Some of the manager's business skills include the following:

- Understanding the organization and the organization's core business
- Understanding marketing, control, contracting, purchasing, law, personnel administration, and the general concept of profitability
- Understanding the concept of direct and indirect cost allocation
- Understanding how to translate business requirements into project and system requirements

But there is now another important component of project management selection that is being practiced in many organizations: choosing project managers who possess high emotional intelligence.

Emotional Intelligence

The information technology and other high-tech industries used to place a premium on high intelligence quotients (IQ) when hiring new people. But these companies have discovered that IQ, although important, is not the most important or best measure of a good project manager or team member. More important is something called emotional intelligence, or emotional quotient (EQ).

Emotional quotient is, loosely defined, the ability of a person to manage his or her emotions as well as the emotions of others. In 1995, Dr. Daniel Goleman, a psychologist, published the international best-seller *Emotional Intelligence: Why It Can Matter More Than IQ*. Dr. Goleman brought together years of research to show that EQ matters twice as much as IQ or technical skills in job success. His studies of more than 500 organizations proved that factors such as self-confidence, self-awareness, self-control, commitment, and integrity create not only more successful employees but also more successful companies.

Why Do Emotions Matter?

Cultural wisdom has taught us that the workplace is not the place for emotions. Reason and logic have been our guides most of our lives, and intelligence is what we have honored. But we all know of high school honor students who have never been able to hold a steady job, while the class cut-up became the unlikely success story. That is because IQ is only one measure of performance, and a very limited one at that.

On some level, we have always recognized that the ability to understand, monitor, manage, and capitalize on our emotions can help us make better decisions, cope with stress and project failures, and interact with others more effectively. Now, thanks to research conducted by Dr. Goleman and others, there is hard data to prove it. Some of the study results are generalized as follows:

- Research on different jobs in a variety of industries worldwide showed that abilities vital for success were trustworthiness, adaptability, and a talent for collaboration—all emotional competencies.

- Corporations seeking MBAs report that the three most desired capabilities they seek are communication skills, interpersonal skills, and initiative.

- The top 10 percent of computer programming performers exceeded average performers in producing effective programs by over 200 percent, and the superstar performers produce even higher percentages. The reason for this astounding performance is that EQ people are better at teamwork, staying late to finish a project, and mentoring coworkers. In short, they don't compete—they collaborate.

- People who score highest on EQ measures rise to the top of corporations. Among other things, these top performers possess more interpersonal skills and confidence than the average employee does.

Defining Emotional Intelligence

Emotional intelligence is much deeper than having good interpersonal skills. It is being aware of and in control of our own emotions while being empathetic enough to perceive and manage the emotions of others. This does not mean controlling other people—it means understanding other people's emotions well enough to lead them to better performance. The competencies of EQ fall into the five groups shown in Exhibit 8-4. Of the five, self-awareness and self-management are the key groups and the ones that are seldom taught as a part of interpersonal skill training. And unlike IQ, emotional intelligence can be learned. Researchers estimate that EQ training takes about five days for a person to learn about his or her own emotional makeup. In one day of training, a person can gain an awareness of what emotional intelligence is and why it matters. In three days, a person can learn specific skills that can be applied right away. But it takes five days to understand one's own emotional makeup, learn the necessary skills, practice the new behaviors, and experience the kind of transformation that can have an impact on the organization.

Organizations are concerned about hiring project managers with high IQs and about providing them with high-quality training without first determining that they also possess high levels of EQ. Not too surprisingly, it is also becoming apparent that there is also a need for project team members—at least the key team members—to possess higher levels of EQ.

But is high EQ the total answer for successful project management? How *do* technical skills fit into the mix?

Technical Skills

There is no question that the successful project manager must possess some level of technical competence in the technical area of the project. The premise that the project manager is technically knowledgeable about the project is important if for no other reason

Exhibit 8-4. Emotional intelligence competencies.

Self-Awareness	• Self-confidence
	• Emotional self-awareness
	• Accurate self-assessment
Self-Management	• Self-control
	• Trustworthiness
	• Conscientiousness
	• Flexibility
	• Goal-oriented
Self-Motivation	• Self-starting
	• Commitment to improving
	• Enthusiasm
	• Persistence
Social Awareness	• Empathy
	• Organizational awareness
	• Service orientation
Social Skills	• Mentoring
	• Leadership
	• Communication
	• Change agent
	• Conflict management
	• Building bonds
	• Teamwork and collaboration

than to gain credibility with the other team members. It is also important that the project manager have some previous management experience within the field as an assistant project manager, project engineer, or functional manager. However, it is not required that the project manager be an expert in the area of the project. In fact, it is better that the project manager not be an expert in the area of the project because "experts" tend not to be open to suggestions or alternative approaches from the rest of the team members. The recommendation is that the project manager be knowledgeable in the field but be a generalist with a broad knowledge of supporting technology, human relations, management, and communication skills.

The senior management of an organization has the responsibility of hiring and training a cadre of project managers. The best companies are the ones that successfully accomplish this task.

Summary

Project selection has become more critical to companies because of changes in the economy, downsizing for efficiency, and generally increased competition. The need for careful attention to project selection by companies focusing on DOD business is particularly important because the government tends to award contracts based on best value—usually meaning lowest cost—after a long and arduous competition among three to ten companies. Best value to the government also means demonstrated management excellence, technical competence, and the ability to meet schedules and budgets even if the short-term cost is greater than the other competitors' costs. So if a company carefully selects only those projects through which they can demonstrate best value—preferably including a lower cost—their chances of winning a contract are increased, and they often become preferred government contractors, which enhances a company's competitive status.

Several project selection tools, both nonnumeric and numeric types, have been discussed in this chapter. The tools presented are meant to be relatively easy to use but yet provide accurate data upon which sound decisions can be made. The key is to use selection tools that provide the most accurate data possible, not just those that provide quick answers. There is nothing wrong in using payback period or rate of return models to get a sense of the viability of a project or to determine the general cash flow requirements. However, relying on these models alone to select a project can lead to disappointment in a project's performance or, worse, complete failure.

As important as selecting the right project is, picking the right project manager may be even more important. Even a "bad" project can realize a certain level of success if it is managed by a skillful and well-qualified project manager. The key to project management selection is finding people who are generalists with broad experience and skills as managers, communicators, mentors, trainers, and coaches.

CHAPTER 9

The Conceptual Phase: Defining the Project

> Man . . . walks up the stairs of his concepts,
> emerges ahead of his accomplishments.
>
> —John Steinbeck
> *The Grapes of Wrath*

How well and how thorough the activities of the project's conceptual or defining phase are done will determine how successful the project will be. In this phase, the project manager is selected, the project is defined against the customer's requirements and specifications, a core project team is assembled to help plan the project, and all the various pieces of the project plan are started. Exhibit 9-1 depicts the major tasks and activities of this phase and who is responsible for them.

Starting a project and getting it working smoothly require an extraordinary amount of definition, planning, and attention to detail. It is a lack of attention to the small things that eventually sidetracks some projects and leaves the project team wondering what happened. Unfortunately, many of us are so anxious to get moving on a project that we jump right into it without giving adequate attention to the up-front definition and planning tasks. It is the old

157

Exhibit 9-1. Conceptual phase tasks, activities, and responsible parties.

Tasks	Activities	Responsibility
Initiate project.	Select project manager.	Senior management.
Analyze and validate the project requirements, specifications, and opportunities.	Assess project opportunity. Develop project scope statement. Review scope with customer.	Project manager.
Assemble core project team.	Review project specifications/requirements to identify key members of project team. Develop benefit-cost analysis. Identify needed resources.	Project manager with functional managers.
Develop high-level project plan.	Define project. Develop technical solution. Develop technical alternatives. Develop high-level WBS. Identify functional responsibilities. Identify stakeholders. Develop cost and schedule estimates. Perform initial risk assessment. Start developing supporting plans.	Project manager and core team members.

| Prepare project charter. | Write project charter. Outline communication requirements. Document project manager's responsibility and authority. Write executive summary. Obtain project approval and go-ahead. | Senior management with project manager. |

"ready, fire, aim" problem; we fire before we aim, or, in this case, we start work before we do the definition and planning. This chapter stresses the importance of project definition and putting together a core team to lay out the basic elements of the project plan.

Initiating the Project

Getting to the point of initiating a project requires considerable analysis by the organization—business case analysis, determination of organizational capabilities, resource availability, and past experience. However, too often the potential project manager is not involved in this crucial phase, and he or she must be prepared to get the information needed to successfully initiate and complete the project.

The Project Manager

Once senior management makes the decision to pursue a project, the first step is to assign a project manager and give this person the authority and responsibility to proceed with the activities of the conceptual phase. This moment when the project is handed off is a critical period for the project manager and for the project. The project manager too often lets the moment pass without obtaining all the information available on the project. Often when a person is informed that he or she is to assume responsibility for a new project, the person walks away too excited—or, in some cases, too stunned—to think to ask penetrating questions about the project. If the project is a result of a contract from outside the organization, there will be significant contractual information available already, such as statements-of-work (SOW) and specifications. But if the project is internal to the organization, there is usually little or no substantive documentation available. The project manager must obtain all the information possible about the project by interviewing the key people who had any part in assessing and selecting the project. Of particular importance is determining who was for and who was against doing the project. (We will discuss the importance of stakeholder support later in this chapter.) The project manager may have to be a pest, but gathering all the basic and defining information at this stage will save a lot of time and headaches later.

The Core Project Team

Any project manager will have a sense of the scope and skills required for the project but usually will not have the expertise to define the project, determine the type and number of people needed for it, write all the necessary supporting plans, develop the schedules, and work out the budget all by him- or herself. That would not be a wise endeavor even for someone who did have that breadth of expertise; working as a team reduces the risk of missing important elements of the project.

Once the project manager has gathered all the basic data, the next step is to form a team to help define and plan the project. This initial team is called the *core project team* or the *plan development team*. The team is composed of experienced people who represent the various functional groups, but they may not be the project team once the project gets under way. At this stage in the project, the project manager's focus is to determine exactly what is to be the final product(s) and how best to accomplish the work. The challenge is to organize a group of subject matter experts who can define the project. The project manager will have to do this with the help and advice of the functional managers. Forming the core team will be the first test of the project manager's negotiation and team-building skills.

Analyzing and Validating the Project Opportunity, Requirements, and Specifications

One reason for project failure is that some organizations do not evaluate their capability to provide the requisite expertise or to allocate the required resources to a project before they begin development. It is crucial to assess the project opportunity and to determine if the project is a good fit for the company's strategic goals, and more important, that the project fits within their capability to perform. There are tools for making this determination.

Assessing Project Opportunity

Every project is an opportunity. But how much of an opportunity? If the project results from winning a competitive contract, the bid price to win the contract may be so low that the company cannot afford to perform. This dilemma occurs more often than one might think because the overriding criterion in a competitive bid is the price. Similarly, internal projects need to be assessed against company goals and costs to determine whether the benefits outweigh the overall costs.

The major tool for assessing project opportunity is a benefit-to-cost analysis, discussed in the previous chapter. Although this analysis is usually done during the project selection process, a new analysis should be done in the conceptual phase to make certain that all the benefits and all the costs are accounted for. As the requirements and specifications are reviewed or developed, it is not unusual to discover that what appeared to be a promising project may just be too costly or too complex for the organization to tackle. Or, on a more optimistic note, it may be that the opportunity is much better than originally thought and many more opportunities may be spawned from this one. In any event, analyzing the opportunity to determine the impact on the organization is required for planning the cash flow, resources, and technology requirements and to provide a basis for approval for project go-ahead. Remember that there are, or should be, go/no-go decision points at various milestones in the project's life cycle, and the end of the conceptual phase is a major one.

Reviewing the Opportunity Alternatives

Assessing the opportunity has built-in advantages other than just determining if the project is viable. This assessment provides the team a chance to look at and develop other approaches to the technical solution. In the process of analyzing the project requirements, corporate capability, and resources, a better way of attacking the project may emerge.

One of the most beneficial results of the opportunity and opportunity alternatives assessment is that there is of necessity a technology assessment as well. It is through this technology assessment that the project manager can begin to make some trade-offs on the materials needed for the project, make-or-buy decisions, and vendor selections. This is the area where cost reductions can occur and schedule improvements can be made. For example, in the technology assessment, it may be determined that an alternative piece of equipment will work just as well as the originally planned item and will cost less. It also might be found that it is more cost-effective and better for the schedule to subcontract some parts of the work, particularly if the parent organization has limited expertise in one or more areas.

The scope management plan is developed as early in the project as possible, usually during the conceptual phase. However, depending on the organization's business process, it actually can be developed earlier—say, during the business analysis review of projects. The scope management plan must be developed before product development begins because this plan is the basis for the product and project baseline definitions. The baseline should never change unless the customer changes the product requirements with an accompanying contract change to account for any schedule and costs impacts. The scope management plan should, however, be reviewed on a continual basis to ensure that all the customer's requirements are being met.

Assessing the opportunity and assessing the opportunity alternatives are not just exercises to make sure all the squares have been checked. Performing these assessments, if done rigorously and in detail, will help the project team optimize the technical approach and usually will uncover ways to improve the cost and schedule profiles.

Developing the Project Scope Statement and Project Charter

Perhaps the most difficult part of the project management process is determining what the customer really wants. I often hear project managers complain that their customers cannot define what the product is to be, what its functions are, and what technology is to be used. Often, the customer does not actually know either, and it becomes an exercise in frustration for both the customer and the project manager to try to scope the project. This lack of definition can increase the cost of the project and can create false starts that affect the schedule.

When I talk about project scope, I mean a description of what the project is suppose to accomplish, how big the product is, how long it will take, what types of skill sets are needed to accomplish the project, and approximately how many resources. In short, the term *scope* defines what is to be done, how it is to be done, and how long it will take. Scope definition is determined from and consists of:

- Requirements definition
- WBS development
- Requirements analysis
- Design, development, and implementation concept development
- Completion criteria, that is, quality requirements definition
- Customer acceptance test procedures definition

Reviewing the Opportunity with the Plan Sponsor

The sponsor of a project is the person, functional group, or organization that will finance the project. The sponsor may or may not be the ultimate customer but is the project manager's primary customer at this stage of the project's life cycle.

Clearly it is important to include the sponsor or customer, whether external or internal to the organization, in the opportunity assessment process. Participation helps customers to refine their own thinking about what they want their projects to accomplish and helps project managers to develop a project's scope. It is far better to help the customer define the project early than to muddle through several iterations to produce something the customer may eventually decide she likes.

Assembling the Core Project Team

The core project team assembled early in the conceptual phase of the project helps with the planning and scope development; these individuals may or may not be a part of the final team. In fact, they usually won't be a member of the project team because the core team often is made up of supervisory-level individuals. They are in positions and possess the expertise to define resource and technical requirements, and therefore to define exactly who should be on the team; however, they usually do not perform the project tasks.

The core team's principal responsibility is to prepare an initial project plan and to establish resource requirements, not to do the actual work. But an ancillary responsibility is to identify those who ultimately will comprise the permanent project team and to get them involved in refining resource, cost, and schedule estimates. Besides, using the project team members at this stage will foster a better understanding of the requirements, and it will be an excellent way to begin building team spirit and commitment. Therefore, it is crucial to identify project team members as early as possible and to identify those who will remain team members until their expertise is no longer required. Frequent team changes tend to reduce morale and project commitment.

Obtaining Resource Commitments

Once the required resources are identified, the real challenge of getting functional management commitment begins. Negotiating for resources will be a constant task of the project manager. That is why negotiating skills rank high on the list of required skills for the successful project manager. (Refer to Chapter 3 for guidance in negotiating with the functional managers.)

The best approach to obtaining the support of functional managers is by showing them how the project will benefit their group. This approach requires the project manager to be prepared to discuss the project in depth. One of the most useful tools for this purpose is a talking paper or short paper that succinctly describes the project. (A talking paper is a one- or two-page paper in a bullet or list format summarizing the subject. It is used in much the same way a speaker uses index cards, hence the name.) I often leave this paper with the functional managers so that they can read it over at their leisure. It is important, though, to have orally described the project in enough detail that it will be easy for the functional manager to agree with the project manager's request.

Knowing Who You Want and Asking for Them

Too many project managers approach the functional groups with a request for resources without identifying specific individuals—a serious mistake, because the tendency is to provide people who are not strong project team members or who have less experience and skill. In other words, the functional manager would much prefer to keep the best staff available for the functional requirements of the group.

The project manager should always approach this task with specific names of the subject matter experts needed. It won't be possible for the functional managers to accommodate the project manager every time because the requested individuals may be committed to other projects already. Nevertheless, by naming specific individuals, the project manager defines the skill level desired from the functional group. The project manager can then take the position that if the requested individuals are not available, someone of the functional manager's choice will suffice as long as the person possesses the same, or better, qualifications. To begin negotiations for less qualified people will guarantee less qualified people.

Assigning Resources to Planning

As each member of the team is identified, he or she should be assigned to developing the project charter and project plan. The project manager's responsibility at this stage is to provide an abbreviated orientation for the project team, make specific assignments for analyzing the requirements and specifications, and begin writing the plans.

There is a lot of pressure on the project manager to get the project rolling. The customer wants to see progress as soon as possible, and the senior managers tend to be impatient for action too. Progress is not progress unless it is visible. Perhaps that is why so many projects get started with inadequate planning. There is no question that it is imperative to get the project moving as quickly as possible, but it is more important to define the project completely and produce a plan that will guide the team to a successful conclusion to the project. It will test the project manager's mettle, but firm resistance, within the realm of good judgment, to the pressure of kicking off the project too soon will pay dividends in the long run.

Developing a High-Level Project Plan

This early in the project, it is difficult to have enough information to write a detailed plan. The objective at this stage is to write a high-level plan that can be used to develop a project charter and to ensure that the customer and the parent organization agree with the requirement definition and the proposed technical approach. That is not to say that a great deal of work is not required; in fact, this part of the project cycle is laying the groundwork for the planning process in the next phase of the project's life cycle.

Stakeholder Analysis

A stakeholder is anyone or any organization that is involved in or may be affected by project activities. In my seminars, I am constantly struck by how many project managers remark, after a discussion about stakeholders, that they could now understand why their project was not completely successful: They had failed to identify the stakeholders and to keep them properly informed about the project.

The project manager and the core team need to identify all the stakeholders as soon as possible. Exhibit 9-2 is a simple form to use in the stakeholder analysis. The form has provisions for indicating whether the stakeholder is for or against the project or is neutral. A stakeholder with negative feelings about a project can scuttle it before the project manager knows what happened. It is absolutely crucial to identify all the stakeholders and determine who has negative feelings and why. The form also has a place to record strategies for winning over negative and neutral stakeholders. The idea is twofold: first, win over the negative stakeholders so that the project efforts won't be sabotaged; and second, change the negative and neutral stakeholders into positive allies.

Most of the time, it is easy to identify stakeholders: the functional manager who supplies the personnel for the project, the customer, and the project manager's direct superior, for example. The difficulty comes when trying to identify individuals or groups who have indirect or downstream involvement with the project—for example, the person or group with the responsibility for maintaining the product after the project to produce it is completed, the conservation group with concerns about how the project's results will affect the environment, and the regulatory agency interested in whether the project meets government standards. The conservation and the regulatory groups do not have direct interests in the project itself, but they do have an interest in how it is administered and what it produces.

Another major purpose of the stakeholder analysis is to determine who needs what kinds of reports. Some stakeholders have no need for and do not care about having status reports more often than, say, quarterly. Some require only high-level overviews of the progress. But others will need to have or will want detailed reports on a frequent basis. The analysis will help the project team to determine what level of detail to provide and how often to provide it.

Exhibit 9-2. Stakeholder analysis form.

STAKEHOLDERS	POSITION			REASON FOR POSITION	STRATEGY TO CHANGE POSITION
	FOR	NEUTRAL	AGAINST		

Evaluating the Requirements

The project manager's major task during this phase is to evaluate and define the requirements. The sources for determining what the requirements are include:

- The project contract (if the project results from a competitive bid)
- The statement of work
- Specifications—that is, product requirements, prepared by the customer
- WBS
- The delivery schedule
- Other documented customer and user inputs

If the project customer is internal to the organization, there will not be a documented specification, or SOW. That is why it is critical for the project manager to determine who in the organization had any part in choosing or creating the project, what the rationale and need are behind the project, and who in the organization supports or does not support the project. In short, the usual onus for developing requirements for an internal project lies more with the project manager and project team than with the customer. Requirements definition is done by answering the questions in Exhibit 9-3, but generally the objective is to determine exactly what is being produced, what its function is, who is going to use it, how it will be integrated into other systems, how long it will take to produce it, and how much it will cost.

When the project team members are satisfied they understand the requirements, the project manager reviews the requirements with the customer to ensure that the team's understanding of what the customer wants agrees with the customer's intent. With customer agreement secured, the project team can now define the project.

Developing the Project Definition

Once the requirements are completely defined and analyzed, defining the project is relatively easy. Developing the project defini-

Exhibit 9-3. Project requirements checklist.

What will the project's final product(s) be?

What is the product's function?

How does the product work?

What are the product's physical characteristics?

What are the product's performance characteristics?

How reliable must the product be, and what are the criteria for determining reliability?

Does the product have to be integrated into other systems?

If the product is to be integrated into other systems, what are the interface requirements?

Who will use the product, and how will it be used?

Does the user have to be trained to operate the product?

Who provides the training for the product? Is training a part of this project?

Who will maintain the product after it is placed in service?

What documentation is required for this product?

tion means agreeing on a technical approach to the project, determining what tasks need to be accomplished and how much they will cost and how long they will take, what the likely problems or risk areas are, and what additional plans have to be written.

A Proposed Technical Solution

The core project team is composed of subject matter experts from the various functional groups of the organization. These experts can best determine the technical solution for the project. The project manager has to guide the process, but it should be a team solution for producing the product.

In many cases, it may be politically wise for the project manager to approach the functional managers for advice and input relative to the technical approach. This approach is particularly helpful if the functional manager does not fully support the project. Most of us are flattered when our advice is sought, and this approach often gains an ally. Also, we often receive solid advice that strengthens the technical approach.

Developing a technical solution should also be a time to assess the potential risk areas and come up with contingency plans to cope with these problems. It is not possible to determine all the risks ahead of time, but from historical data, it is certainly possible to identify the problems that similar projects had and to plan for them. Many project managers fail to plan for these contingencies and have to deal with them in a reactive manner rather than having plans in place that allow for a proactive approach to risk.

A High-Level WBS

The WBS is the most important tool of the project manager because all the other tools can be developed from it. At this stage, though, about the best we can do is a high-level WBS—that is, to the second or, better, the third level. It may be possible to develop the WBS to a lower level if the project is similar to previous ones done by the organization. Although there is no WBS that applies to all projects, it is certainly feasible to create a WBS template using applicable boilerplate material. For instance, certain functions, such as the project management function and documentation procedures and publication, are nearly the same for each project. Then the WBS can be tailored to the individual project. The major objective here is to develop the WBS to a level that will allow the project manager to identify functional responsibilities and a reasonably good estimate of cost and schedule.

Functional Responsibilities

The project manager must always remember that the functional groups and the functional managers are responsible for accomplishing the technical solution to the project. This means that the project manager has the oversight responsibility to see that the project is accomplished in accordance with the customer's requirements, but the functional staff actually does the work. Hence, it is crucial that the project requirements be defined completely so that each required task is identified. That is the major purpose of the high-level WBS. Once the functional requirements are identified, the project manager can start the negotiating process for these resources.

Cost and Schedule Estimates

The WBS is not a schedule, but all the elements needed to develop the schedule are contained within it. As the WBS is developed, each task and subtask unfolds so that the project requirements, functional responsibilities, and individual subject matter expert requirements are identified. Once the WBS is developed to a level low enough to designate it as a work package and to identify an individual to do the work, then schedules and budgets can be determined. Also, when the WBS is completely defined, task interdependencies can be determined, and a network analysis can be performed.

High-Level Risk Assessment

There has been a growing awareness of the susceptibility of projects to risk and the need to manage risk consciously. It may seem to be a given that project managers closely monitor and manage risk. The fact is, though, risk is usually considered to be negative, and in the past, the corporate environment of many organizations did not encourage reporting risks or potential risks. Too many senior managers were not open to bad news, and risks were categorized as bad.

In the late 1980s, risk became recognized as something normal in every project, and rather than trying to hide the potential for it, project managers now identify and manage it. Furthermore, risk is no longer viewed as a pure loss situation; it is viewed equally as an opportunity. *Risk management* is a process of identifying the risk, determining whether there is opportunity or loss potential with it, and planning ways to handle it. The identification of risk has to start in the conceptual phase in order to define the technical solution, determine make-or-buy strategies, and make plans insomuch as possible to deal with the risk.

Naturally, all risks cannot be identified at this stage of the project. The project manager and the initial team have to rely on experience and historical data to identify what risks might be experienced. Exhibit 9-4 shows a simple form for risk identification. The form is divided into three broad categories of budget, schedule, and performance or quality, since these are the three major

Exhibit 9-4. Risk assessment form.

RISK AREA	POTENTIAL PROBLEM	WHEN AND HOW IT COULD OCCUR	ALTERNATIVE ACTION
Budget			
Schedule			
Quality			

elements of the project that a project manager is concerned with. These categories can be further divided into specialized categories to fit the individual project. Bear in mind that at this stage, we are concerned with a high-level risk assessment for planning purposes, but risk will be considered in greater detail in the planning phase and will receive continuous attention throughout the project's life cycle.

Supporting Project Plans

The final step in the initial project planning stage is to develop supporting plans that serve to keep the project running smoothly, inform stakeholders and project team members of progress, and provide a baseline for meeting the technical specifications. Supporting plans range from fairly simple and straightforward matrices that show who receives progress or status reports and the level of information to be portrayed to very detailed and complex documents that show what the level of reliability of a product is and how to measure it. Generally, each project has a technical plan showing the general approach, a communication plan showing who receives what type of status reports and how often, a project review plan, a technical performance measurement plan(s), and resource allocation plans. These plans are part of the overall project management plan and are either embedded in the master plan or, if fairly large and complex, attached as appendixes. A rule of thumb about planning and the depth of plans is to plan to a level of detail that is commensurate with the amount of monitoring and control needed. Extremely careful monitoring and control requirements need very detailed plans; for periodic monitoring and relatively little control from the project manager, high-level planning will suffice.

It is important to remember that all plans, particularly the scope management plan, should be monitored continuously and changed in accordance with preagreed change control processes. Generally, there are two change control processes set up for project changes: one is a contractual process defined by the buyer to allow changes to the product definition (this is especially important for those projects that don't have well-defined requirements at the beginning), and the other is a process whereby the provider of the product can recommend changes to the customer as the product definition and implementation matures. For example, most products benefit from value analyses, which show that certain functionality is not really required and can save money if not incorporated. In either case, it is crucial that *all* changes be agreed on by the customer and documented in a formal contract change. Otherwise, the provider of the product will have to "eat" the costs in a firm-fixed-price contract, the contract of choice in today's competitive market.

Preparing the Project Charter

The culmination of the conceptual phase is to prepare a *project charter,* which is a document, prepared by senior management in conjunction with the project manager, that briefly outlines the project scope, names the project manager, identifies the required resources, and establishes the communication plan for the project. The charter is the primary vehicle for identifying the parameters of the project and can be a powerful communication and negotiation tool. It is the vehicle for obtaining buy-in from the functional managers and for obtaining final approval to continue with the project. Exhibit 9-5 provides a general outline for a charter.

As important and useful as charters are, very few organizations require or use them. Perhaps it is because there is a lack of understanding about project management and project management procedures, or perhaps many organizations view the project management plan as the charter. Whatever the reason, it is in the project manager's best interest to push for a project charter because it

Exhibit 9-5. Project charter outline.

I.   Purpose

II. Project Establishment

III. Project Manager Designation and Authority

IV. Project Manager Responsibility
    A. Support organizations' responsibilities
    B. Project organization and structure
    C. Project team composition

V.   Project Initiation
    A. Formal project plan
    B. Approved budgets
    C. Approved plan

VI. Project Personnel
    A. Assignments to projects
    B. Reporting structure
    C. Performance appraisals

VII. Communication Plan

VIII. Definitions

IX. Appendixes

---

establishes his or her authority and provides the parameters for the project, including an estimate of resources. The project charter provides the project manager with additional leverage when negotiating with the functional managers because in all likelihood, they will have been a part of the charter preparation and will already have agreed, or, at the minimum, be on notice that they have an obligation, to support the project.

A charter is not required if the project results from a contract outside the organization because the contractual documents, along with the original proposal, serve as the charter. Otherwise, the project manager should always push to have a charter developed. Remember that the project manager and the initial project team will provide most of the input that comprises the charter, but senior management is responsible for preparing the final document.

After the project charter is completed and final approval to go ahead with the project is obtained, the project manager is ready to assemble the full project team and kick off the project. Their first priority is to finalize the project plan, organize the project team, and prepare to implement the project.

Summary

The conceptual phase of the project is the defining phase. During this phase, the project manager puts together a core project team, and together they define the project. The project definition requires a complete understanding of the requirements, the technical skills needed, the personnel and capital resource needs, and who has a vested interest in the project. Attention to detail is probably more critical in this phase than in any other phase of the project.

A project charter is a document prepared by senior management with input from the project manager. This document provides the authority to the project manager to run the project, and it delineates the responsibilities of the various supporting groups of the organization. It also outlines the team members' responsibilities and reporting chain. Many companies don't bother with developing a charter. However, it is in the best interest of the project manager to push for one because it will provide a certain amount of leverage when he or she has to negotiate for resources.

For projects won on a competitive basis—that is, there is a formal contracting document associated with the project—the contract itself serves as the charter. Nevertheless, it is much cleaner and clearer to have a separate document that addresses project policy and philosophy. A charter should be a routine part of the project initiation process. It protects the project manager as well as the organization.

CHAPTER 10

Project Management in Different Organizational Environments

Management means getting things done through
the active support of other people.

—HAROLD KERZNER
professor of Systems Management, Baldwin-Wallace College, Berea, Ohio

Virtually every book on project management includes a section on organizational structures, and they all discuss the three most common structures: functional or traditional, project management, and matrix. To be sure, these are the three basic organizational structures on which all other structures are modeled. In my experience, though, there are two additional organizational concepts that deserve attention.

The fact is that few organizations are organized in one of the ideal forms. They are a mixture of two or more of the three basic types, or they are a variation of one of them. Also, I have observed that in every single one of my project management classes, there has been at least one student who works in a "nonorganizational" organization or a start-up company not yet large enough to need a formal organizational structure.

Why Understanding Organizational Structures Is Important

The project manager has no influence on the way a company is organized. So why is it important to study and understand organizational structures? There are actually several important reasons why every project manager needs to understand organizational structures:

1. Each organizational structure imposes its own unique advantages and disadvantages relative to the ease of managing a project.

2. The project manager will have greater success interfacing with management, stakeholders, and functional groups if he or she understands the relationship of each to the project.

3. In those many instances when the project manager has to negotiate for resources, understanding the organizational structure will allow him or her to maneuver through the intricate maze of responsibility and authority lines.

4. Organizational structures apply to more than the project manager's organization. The project manager is also responsible for interfacing with the customer, vendors, and other company team members. All of these entities have their own unique organizational structures, and understanding the other person's organization will make dealing with them easier.

5. Since today's workforce is nomadic and most markets are extremely dynamic, it is absolutely certain that every project manager will experience several different organizational structures during his or her career, even if he or she stays in the same company.

Types of Organizational Structures

There are three basic types of organizational structures: the functional or traditional (hereafter referred to as the functional organization), project management, and matrix. Also, there are the nonorganizational organizations and the mixture of the basic three types, usually that of functional and matrix organization. In addition, many organizations have adopted the project, or program, management office (PMO) structure that operates within any of the basic organizational models. (The PMO is discussed in some detail in Chapter 11.)

Functional Organization

The functional organization is the oldest of the organizational types. It was "invented" by the Roman army and was the structural design model of choice until the mid-1900s. This organization worked well, and still does, as long as the business is not complex or diverse and the company does not compete in a dynamic market. Manufacturing or engineering companies often are organized in this fashion.

The functional organization is one that is organized along core competency or functional lines. The structure is well-known and follows the general form of the example in Exhibit 10-1.

When a company is organized along functional lines, each proj-

Exhibit 10-1. Functional or traditional organization.

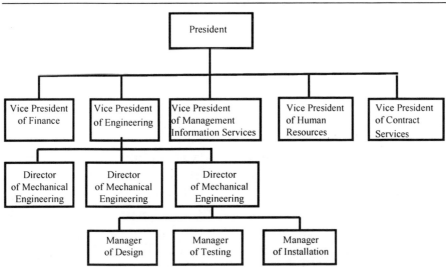

ect is matched with the functional group that has the greatest interest in seeing it successfully completed. That is, a mechanical engineering project would be placed in the mechanical engineering group, an electrical engineering project would be placed in the electrical engineering group, and so on. There are a number of advantages for project management in this type of organizational hierarchy:

1. Most functional groups contain the requisite technical capability to accomplish the project, and the functional organization accommodates the flexibility required to access this expertise.

2. Individual experts can support a number of different projects of the same class or type.

3. There isn't a loss of technical expertise when a person leaves the company. That is, because the technical expertise can be grouped and shared within the function, there remains a continuous technical base even as various experts change jobs and move out of the group or company.

4. The functional organization historically has been the path of career advancement for those members who have expertise in the functional area. Therefore, team members always have a feeling of home even after the project ends.

As logical and straightforward as this sounds, there is a price to pay for being functionally organized:

1. The customer is not the focus of the project manager's concern. Often the functional arrangement places several levels of management between the project manager and the customer, particularly an external customer. Even when there are not many layers of management between the project manager and the customer, the project manager's primary focus is on the activities and requirements of the functional group rather than on the project requirements.

2. It is not always clear who is in charge of the project. The project manager's functional superior often interjects him- or herself into the project, thus causing confusion within the project team and leaving conflicting directions about the project work.

3. Since the project tends not to be in the mainstream of the functional life, there is usually a lot of difficulty in motivating the project team. Often the performance goals of the team members do not include project work. Hence, there is less interest in achieving the project goals. In fact, the team member may view the project assignment as a secondary duty.

4. If the project is large and complex, requiring expertise from other functional areas, it is difficult to obtain the coordination and teamwork required to accomplish the task, and it is virtually impossible to design, build, or manage the project from a holistic perspective.

5. Functional organizations tend to foster internal competition among the functional groups to the extent of creating a lack of teamwork or a noncooperative atmosphere among team members.

Project Organization

From the perspective of the project manager, the project organizational structure is the best possible organization to work in. From the perspective of the corporation, it can be one of the worst.

The pure project organization is one that organizes around each of its projects. That is, each project has assigned to it all the requisite skills, technical and administrative, needed to accomplish the work. This type of organization is depicted in Exhibit 10-2.

The project organization is good for both the project manager and the project for several reasons:

1. There is no doubt about who is charge of the project. The project manager has total responsibility for the project and the people and resources assigned to it.

Exhibit 10-2. The project organization.

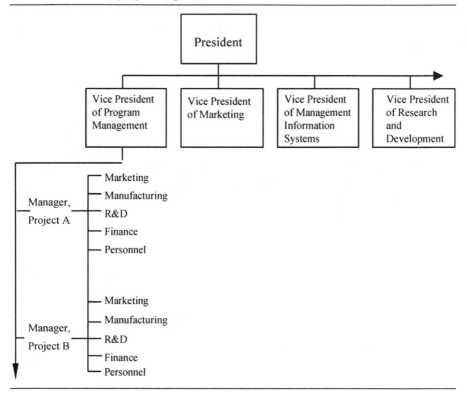

2. The project manager has functional or line responsibility for the people working on the project.

3. The project is customer-focused. The project manager can make instantaneous decisions about the project and can react immediately to any customer changes.

4. There is a unity of command. That is, the project's team members report to only one boss.

5. If the project is one that elicits a strong identity, the team members usually develop a strong commitment to it and the project manager.

6. The project management organizational structure supports a holistic approach to the project.

As strong as the project organization concept is, there are some equally strong reasons why it does not work for every organization:

1. When the company is project-driven and has several active projects at any given time, the duplication of completely staffing each project is a financial drain.

2. Duplicating the support functions (administrative, legal, contractual, human resources, and marketing) drives the overhead costs so high that the company will become non-competitive in the market.

3. A project team that is not in the functional mainstream tends to ignore company policies and procedures and can create severe long-term problems with their customers. A customer might not like the way it is treated on a succeeding project if it was accustomed to having the previous project team cut corners for it.

4. Project managers in a project organization tend to keep technical expertise on the payroll after they finish their tasks because they don't want to lose the expertise. And the project manager will hire technical expertise against the time they will be needed just to ensure their availability.

5. If the project is long and has high visibility, it tends to take on a life of its own. Although that is good for morale and camaraderie, it can be very difficult for the project manager to bring it to closure. The team members don't want the project to end and may sabotage the effort to conclude the project.

Matrix Organization

With the functional and project management structures on the opposite ends of the organizational spectrum, a new concept of organizing for success was needed. The matrix organization is an attempt to mitigate the disadvantages of the functional and project organizations while capitalizing on the advantages of both. The result, an overlay of the project organization onto the functional organization, is shown in Exhibit 10-3. The addition of the program management function places a project advocate in the organizational hierarchy on a par with the other functional leadership.

The numbers against each of the projects in Exhibit 10-3 refer to the amount of time per week (or month) required of a person from each of the functional areas. That is, a marketing person is needed to work on Project 1 for one-and-a-half days per week. Four days of marketing support is needed for Project 2. Note that the same person may support two or more different projects.

The advantages of the matrix organization are:

1. The project is the emphasis, and the customer is the focus.
2. The project team can draw from the functional technical expertise across the organization. This arrangement is even better than in a project organization because of a larger technical base.
3. The project team can draw from the support staff as needed without having to maintain its own. The corporate support staff can support many different projects without duplicating staff functions.
4. It is generally easier for the company to balance resources even if there are several active projects.

The matrix organization has significant advantages over the other two forms; nevertheless, there are still some serious disadvantages:

1. The strength or weakness of the project is a direct function of the strength of the project manager. If the project manager is a strong manager and commands the respect and authority of the functional managers, the project will take on the characteristics of the project management organization. Otherwise, it tends to look like a project in a functional organization. This balance can be very fragile.

Exhibit 10-3. Matrix organization.

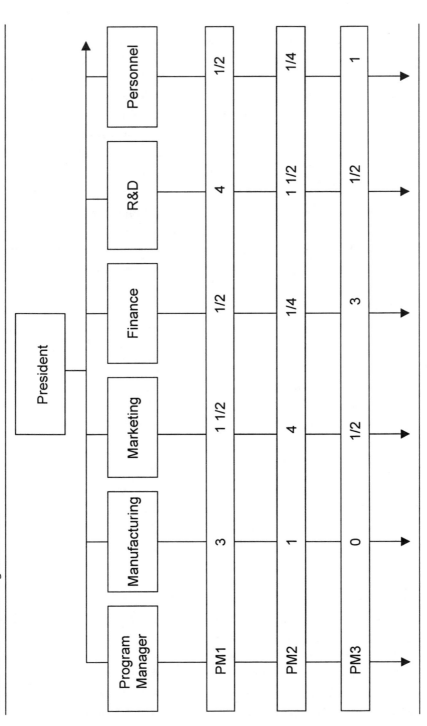

2. The matrix concept violates the unity of command. That is, the team members report to the project manager for project direction and are responsible to him or her for accomplishing the project's goals, but they still work for a functional manager. Maintaining the proper balance and perspective in this relationship can be difficult for both the project manager and the team members. The team member's loyalty will always be first with the functional boss, who writes the performance reports.

3. Projects in the matrix concept tend to have serious problems when it becomes time to terminate them. (This is the same problem that occurs in a project organization.) Team members may block project termination because of the fear that they won't have a functional home to return to once the project ends.

4. Strangely enough, it is not always clear who is in charge in a matrix organization. It happens occasionally that the director or vice president of program management interposes him- or herself into the project. Also, if the project manager isn't careful, the functional managers will assert themselves as the driving force behind the project.

Mixed Organizations

In reality, there are few pure functional, project, or even matrix organizations. Most organizations are a mixture of two or more of these types. Even when a company strives to organize along the lines of a matrix organization, the strength of the project manager determines whether the project operates as it would in a functional or project organization. If the pure functional concept is at one end of the organizational spectrum and the pure project concept is at the other, then the pure matrix concept is halfway between the two. But if the project manager is strong, in terms of representing the project forcefully when dealing with the functional hierarchy, the project tends to operate or take on the appearance of the project organization. And if the project manager tends to be weaker and subjugates him- or herself to the functional manager, the project takes on the characteristics of the functional organization. These are some of the ways organizations appear to be hybrid or mixed organizations.

Other organizations consciously mix types of organizational structures within the overall framework of the company. For instance, a large corporation may be structured along functional lines at the top levels but in a project or matrix or mixture of the two in the various profit centers. This often happens where the corporation has separate subsidiaries within the company's holdings. It almost always happens in entrepreneurial companies when they first begin, particularly if they are in a services market or have a diverse customer base. The corporate headquarters will be functionally organized while the rest of the company is divided into profit centers that essentially operate as little stand-alone companies. These profit centers take on an organizational structure that meets their immediate customer needs.

Since there are so many variations for organizational structures, one would think that any company could organize to meet its customers' needs while running smoothly and efficiently and providing employees with the kind of atmosphere they need to grow. Yet, we hear frustrations and complaints expressed every day from managers and employees alike about the lack of flexibility of their company or about the difficult environment in which they work. The problem is that changing an organizational structure is not easy. In theory, it is easy, and on paper it is easy. But the theory or the new organizational lines on paper cannot account for the culture of the organization.

On average, it takes about five years to make a radical change in a company's organization and to get to the goals that prompted the change. It takes that long to change the company's culture. There has to be a buy-in by all that the new organization is a better way to do business and take care of the employees' needs than the old organization could manage. Engineering such a major cultural change requires extraordinary leadership from the senior management. Unfortunately, many senior managers lack the special training or knowledge about how to accomplish a cultural shift and to mold a new thinking and action process.

What happens all too often when a decision is made to change the organization is that the senior management directs the functional groups to operate in a cooperative and team-spirited way without making any substantive changes in the structure or the way daily tasks are managed. In other words, the idea is to make a functional organization operate like a matrix organization by directing the functional groups to start cooperating cross-functionally or across the company's horizontal lines. This approach to a hybrid organization works well if the functional groups can cooperate in a team-spirited way. If they don't, it only worsens any existing problems. The project manager still has to run the project the same as he or she would in a functional organization.

Nonorganizational Organization

The classes I teach in project management are geared toward working adults, generally at the midpoint in their careers. Therefore, all of them have experience in the workplace. In every single class, there is at least one, and usually more, who have never worked in anything but a very small company. Invariably, the discussion about organizational structures reveals that some of these people have difficulty relating to anything in the discussion because their company actually has no formal organization. This nonorganizational concept is not uncommon. The typical entrepreneurial start-up company has no formal structure, sometimes for years. These companies tend to operate on the strength of the personality of the owner, and the owner tends to make all the day-to-day decisions. This pattern continues until the company grows so big that the owner cannot attend to all the daily decisions, the employees become frustrated because they cannot get timely decisions needed to do their jobs, and there are difficulties with recruitment, employee benefits, and work space. Finally, it is decided that the company has to have a formal structure. Until that occurs, though, no one really worries or even thinks about staff or line functions.

There are some advantages to running a project in a small company that isn't formally organized:

1. The organization is very flexible, and getting to the top management is usually easy.

2. The project tends to be focused on the customer.

3. Everyone in the organization tends to pitch in wherever they are needed.

4. Morale is usually high because the company operates like one big family.

As nice as working in a small company sounds, there can be some horrendous disadvantages:

1. These small companies most often do not have sufficient staff to do all that is necessary or, more to the point, all that they have to do to keep the business afloat.

2. Depending on what phase of growth or size, the owner may not be as available as the project demands.

3. Because small companies tend to be cash-limited, the best expertise or technology may not be available to the project manager.

4. Almost everyone in the company is overworked.

Summary

The project manager must have a good understanding of organizational types and structures. Each type of organization imposes its own set of advantages and disadvantages on the project and the project manager. Understanding these advantages and disadvantages helps the project manager maximize his or her ability to maneuver through the corporate hierarchy maze to accomplish the goals of the project. Even project managers who work in what I call nonorganizational organizations have to deal with vendors, teammates, or customers who have formal organizational structures. Understanding the customer's organization can shed light on how long it might take to get approval for changes in the project or who the stakeholders are in the customer hierarchy. The project manager can then plan accordingly. He or she is now in a position to plan for demands that are placed on the project's schedule, for instance, that are a result of the customer's organizational peculiarities.

CHAPTER 11

The Project Management Office

For the things we have to learn before we can do them,
we learn by doing them.

—ARISTOTLE
(384–322 B.C.)
from *Diogenes Laertius*

The concept of a project management office (PMO) is not new; it is an old idea with a new life because of the need to manage projects more efficiently—especially information technology (IT) projects. Although PMOs are useful for managing and supporting other types of projects, IT organizations have struggled to deliver projects on time and within budget more than any others. In the mid-1990s, approximately 80 percent of all IT projects failed, and of those that were restarted, about 50 percent failed. Therefore, the challenge to manage projects more closely has caused a resurgence of PMO implementations.

A PMO is not a panacea for all project challenges, because there is no simple recipe for project success. A survey in June 2003 by *CIO Magazine* and PMI® found that PMOs do not give organizations quick fixes and quantifiable savings or easy-to-use cost-saving benchmarks and performance metrics. Interestingly, 74 percent of the respondents to the survey also reported that lower cost was not a benefit of their PMOs.[1]

There are two basic PMO models: The first model acts in a consulting role to provide project managers with training, guidance, and best practice information, while the second model is centralized to maintain staff project managers who run projects for the organization. This chapter discusses the functions of these two PMO models and how they differ, how PMOs are initially set up and maintained, and what the benefits and disadvantages of PMOs are.

PMO Functions and Activities

There are only two basic PMO models, but there are many variations of the content of these models—that is, the extent of the functions and activities within these model structures. There are numerous functions that can describe any given PMO unit, which will differ across organizations and the planned use of the PMO. However, there are five core functions of any PMO:[2]

1. Practice management
2. Infrastructure management
3. Resource integration
4. Technical support
5. Business alignment

One of the difficulties in grasping the concept of PMOs is coming to grips with the best model for an organization—which model is most appropriate for obtaining organizational goals—and what the relationship is between PMOs and a project manager—that is, who is in charge of the project.

To answer these questions requires a more detailed look at PMO functions than just the five core ones, as well as some of the activities of each function.

An explanation of PMO functions, including those of a centralized model, is a clearer approach for organizational planning—in terms of establishing an appropriate PMO structure—because it allows management the opportunity to determine which functions are most important to them for meeting organizational goals and objectives and whether a centralized or a consultative type model best meets the organization's needs.

The Activities of the PMO

Each of the PMO function activities will be explained, but some of them are self-explanatory. Six of the activities—project governance, resource management, project portfolio management, customer relationships, project recovery, and business performance—may appear to the project manager as being his or her responsibility or the responsibility of another specialized group—that is, not the responsibility of a PMO.

Project Management Methodology. Arguably, this activity is one of the two most important activities of the PMO or any organization attempting to foster a project management environment (the second most important activity is project management tools, discussed later). Without a sound project management methodology to establish policies and procedures, training, and clearly defined operating expectations for the project managers and their teams, any attempt to establish a project management process for managing business is bound to fail.

Developing and establishing a project management methodology requires a thorough analysis of how projects currently are managed in the organization and how they could be better managed. Then, a set of policies and procedures are developed and implemented to achieve the improvements in project management practices. It then becomes the PMO's responsibility to ensure that the methodology is kept current and updated when needed—that is, to manage the methodology as the organization matures.

Project Governance. This activity defines the PMO structure because it is during this activity that the organization determines whether the PMO will function in a consultative role or as a centralized entity. If the former, the project manager uses the PMO as a consultative resource; if the latter, the project manager is essentially on the PMO staff and is assigned to projects as they occur.

The key to establishing an effective and efficient PMO is the charter for its operation. The charter will clearly state who is in charge of the PMO, what the limits of the PMO's authority are, and how the PMO will function relative to the rest of the organization. Other components of this activity include establishing an executive control board, defining reporting lines, relationships of functional groups to the PMO, how project managers are chosen, the limits of their authority, and the alignment of the business activities with project management to ensure that business goals are met.

Resource Management. If the PMO is centralized, resource management is a major part of its responsibility and one that relieves a heavy burden from the project manager. Project managers constantly negotiate for resources, and they usually do not control them—that is, functionally—when they are assigned to the project. So the idea that the PMO actually manages the required resources across several simultaneous projects relieves the project manager of that responsibility, at least to a degree; the project manager still has to negotiate for the numbers and skill sets needed, but he or she can deal directly with the PMO and not with the functional managers, as the case would be with a consultative or no PMO.

Mentoring. Regardless of the PMO model, mentoring is a key responsibility and one that adds significant value to the organization. The reason is simple: A structured process is established and managed that ensures a learning and maturing environment for the organization's project managers. The challenge of a mentoring program is finding qualified mentors who have not only the expertise but also the skills and traits required of good mentors—for example, coaching, communication, listening, knowing the organization, political savvy, or influencing ability.

Project Portfolio Management. This activity traditionally has been performed by a senior management committee. With the advent of centralized PMO organizations, the responsibility for portfolio management is beginning to shift. On the surface, the PMO might not seem the appropriate manager of a company's portfolio of projects. But given that a key to business success is to first choose projects that fit the company's capabilities and expertise and then to align these projects so that they support the company's business goals and strategies, it becomes clear why the PMO is best suited for portfolio management. The primary challenge in assigning the portfolio management responsibility to the PMO is gaining the support of senior management to buy into the concept and to empower the PMO to do the job.

Project Management Tools. The second most important function of the PMO is providing the project manager with the appropriate tools with which to do the project's work. It accomplishes nothing to write procedures and establish methodology if appropriate tools are not available. This activity is a continuing one of evaluating and selecting tools. On the other hand, caution is required not to change tools, particularly software tools, just because a new one becomes available—the key is to evaluate and implement tools that add value to the projects and the organization.

Assessment. Most of the responsibility of any PMO involves constantly assessing the health of projects, competencies, and project and organizational capabilities. Assessments also include performing project audits. But perhaps the most important assessment is that of determining project maturity within the organization—that is, determining whether the organization is realizing an improvement of its project management capability.

Training and Education. Project managers are responsible for training project team members to the extent of their capability and time. Most organizations now have training programs that provide both the project manager and the team with training opportunities. PMOs can also formalize and structure training so that project teams can continue to improve their project management knowledge base. The training is focused on project management concepts, tools, and techniques, but other ancillary skills such as communication, leadership, and negotiation are also taught.

Planning Support. Planning is the crux of project success because it is during this project phase that requirements are defined and technical approaches are developed to accomplish the project's goals. Most projects fail because of an inadequate definition of the requirements by the customer or a misinterpretation of the requirements that are provided. So being able to tap into the expertise of the PMO for planning support is of tremendous value to the project manager. First, this support provides additional experienced, and usually senior, project managers to help ferret out the requirements, particularly if they are poorly written, and second, the PMO, once well established, will provide access to similar project lessons learned.

Customer Relationships. Often, project managers are not the primary interface with the customer. If the primary interface is between a vice president and the customer, for example, the layers of management between the vice president and the project manager can impede the project's progress—at least, it can slow decision making and management instructions. However, with the PMO responsible for customer relations, as is the case in the centralized PMO model, the communication levels between the customer and the project manager are greatly reduced.

Standards and Metrics. It is easy to understand the need for applying standards to project management or to any other aspect of an organization's operations. It is simply that standards have to be set and met in order for consistent quality operations to occur. Too many organizations do not realize the importance of identifying and collecting metrics—perhaps because too few organizations understand what metrics are and what their importance is to continued and improved growth. Metrics, apparently, mean different things to different people. The simple view of "metrics" is that project managers specifically—and organizations in general—need to collect specific data to improve things such as schedule and budgeting techniques, risk analysis, change management, and any other variables that can affect project time and cost estimates.

Metrics are most valuable in improving *any* project estimating models or techniques. So if the PMO can focus on collecting and measuring specifically identified metrics, they can be applied across the organization to better determine accurate budget, schedule, and resource allocation needs. Generally, the project manager is responsible for this activity, but it is clear that PMO organization can dramatically improve this effort.

Organization and Structure. Conceptually, this activity is simple: Set up the PMO structure, establish what the project management structure will be, and ensure stakeholder participation. The problem is that early in the process the organization is struggling with what type of PMO structure they want or will support (consultative or centralized), so the first order of business is to determine the PMO structure. This dilemma is compounded by the view of the project management roles and responsibilities. If, for example, the organization's senior management is from a more traditional approach—that is, project managers are responsible for *all* aspects of the project—the trend of management will be toward a consultative role for the PMO. However, if the organization's senior management is more open to change, and pushing responsibility downward— that is, empowering people or organizations to be responsible for the core business of the company—the organization may be more inclined to embrace a centralized PMO perspective, which changes the traditional role of the project manager. In any event, it is incumbent on senior management to decide at this point which PMO model is best for their view of the company's business prospects.

Career Development. One important function of any PMO is the establishment and implementation of a formal career development program. Career development is more focused on helping project managers and team members to plan a career path, which includes various suggestions for training—that is, types and content of training courses—as well as providing support toward obtaining professional certifications. Many organizations design their career advancement program so that the aspiring project manager earns the recognition and title only after completing the career plan and the project management professional (PMP) certification.

Project Auditing. One of the least favorite things project team members want to hear is that their project is going to be audited. Audits are necessary for a project's success because it is through audits that the project manager and team members can determine the true health of the project. Intellectually, everyone realizes the importance and necessity of audits, but the reality is that most people dread them because of the fear (usually unfounded) that the purpose of audits is to fix blame for any project problems. The audit team must be from outside the project to provide objectivity, but the notion of an outside team often heightens team member anxiety.

The PMO is in the perfect position to alleviate a great deal of this stress while accomplishing the real purpose of an audit. First, the PMO staff is known to all team members. Hence, the auditors are outside the project itself, but they are not viewed as "outsiders." Second, audits by the PMO staff are expected because they are known to be a part of their duties—that is, PMO staff duties are routinely updated and published to all project teams. Finally, with each project team being so closely aligned with the PMO, it will be common knowledge that audits are performed periodically and on a routine basis.

Vendor/Contractor Relationships. Project managers traditionally have managed vendors and other contractors. Every project management plan has a section dealing with how this function will be controlled with the project structure. Often the project manager assumes the responsibility, but in large or complex projects there may be a team member who is specifically designated as the subcontract manager. If the PMO is consultative, this model for subcontract management is likely to continue, possibly with some support—or at least advice—from the PMO.

But if the PMO is centralized, then all vendor and other contract management activities become a part of that office.

This concept has many advantages over that of the project teams being responsible for managing subcontracts, especially for large projects. The PMO can devote resources to subcontract management that otherwise may not be available to the project; the project manager can devote his or her attention to developing the project's product and the myriad administrative tasks that consume his or her energy and time; the PMO can be staffed with specialty skills—for example, legal or contract specialists—that do not typically report to the project manager; the same PMO staff is able to serve as subcontract managers for more than one project at a time—an efficient use of resources; and the PMO staff is in a better position to cultivate a broader base of customer support for current and future projects.

Project Knowledge Management. Knowledge management is hard to define precisely and simply because it requires defining *knowledge* itself. But a reasonable definition for project management can be viewed as a business activity with the two goals of treating the knowledge component of business activities as an explicit concern of business reflected in strategy, policy, and practice at all levels of the organization and of making a direct connection between an organization's intellectual assets—both recorded and personal experience—and positive business results.

Organizations need to manage knowledge for many business and project reasons, such as the following:

- Increased marketplace competitiveness
- Reductions in staffing create the need to replace informal knowledge with formal methods
- Reductions in staffing reduce workforce that holds valuable business and project management knowledge
- Amount of time available to experience and acquire knowledge has diminished

- Mobility of workforce leads to loss of knowledge
- Increasing complexity as businesses become global
- Changes in strategic direction can result in the loss of knowledge (or need for new knowledge) in a specific area.

In short, managing knowledge represents the primary opportunity for achieving substantial savings, significant improvements in human performance, and competitive advantage, all of which are key goals of a PMO.

Facilities and Equipment Support. Obtaining facilities and equipment for a project are seldom problems in the early stages of a project because they are either part of a contract and therefore are identified and funded, or, if the project originates inside the organization, the facilities and equipment are likely supplied. The problem in both cases occurs after the project starts and more facilities and equipment are needed than originally anticipated, or maintenance of either has a lower priority than that of other projects. The PMO is in a better position to balance these resources across multiple projects and to negotiate with senior stakeholders and other functional managers for what is needed. Again, a primary benefit to the project manager is that he or she is relieved from the added burden of performing this task.

Team Development. The primary PMO function for this activity is the actual formation of the project team, which is usually the project manager's responsibility (in some organizations the team is formed—or appointed—by a functional manager, particularly in traditional or functional organizations). There are two advantages of a PMO assuming this function: It relieves the project manager of having to negotiate with several different functional managers for the requisite skill sets, and the PMO can better set up virtual teams or other teams needing specialized equipment and support. In the first case (negotiating for team members), the PMO will have information about what is needed for a particular project and who is available as other projects progress from one phase to another. Second, setting up the physical requirements to support virtual and specialized teams requires specialized skills, which the individual project managers may not possess.

Team development in this context has more to do with the physical and technical aspects of teams than with team member relationships—it is solely the project manager's responsibility to ensure good team communication, interpersonal cohesiveness, and team member development.

Project Recovery. A special set of project team skills and experience is required to recover troubled projects. Once it becomes clear that a project is likely to fail, the original project manager and team are unlikely to effect a reversal because they tend not to be as sensitive to the problems, and one or more of the team (even the project manager) may be the root cause of the potential project failure. Hence, it is best to form a separate team to assess the problems rapidly and to begin recovery. Once the project reaches a "troubled" state, it can never be recovered to its original baseline, which is why a specialized recovery team trained to get as much value from the project as possible is needed.

Since it is expensive to maintain trained and experienced project recovery teams, organizations are relying on PMOs for this function—that is, maintaining a cadre of highly skilled recovery teams that also can function as day-to-day project management teams.

Business Performance. Whether an organization is successful is a function of how well it selects projects that support its strategic and business goals and how well it implements a process for ensuring that these projects maintain their value. Organizations that established a system of portfolio management for monitoring a project's viability (without first establishing a PMO) are discovering that the PMO is the perfect entity for this purpose.

Because the PMO has oversight responsibility for all projects in the organization, the PMO staff can monitor the health of each project and whether a project is contributing to the organizational needs and goals. What is especially important about having a centralized function for monitoring projects is that monitoring—and control when necessary—becomes near real time, which is particularly important in a fast-changing competitive market. The PMO fills this responsibility.

PMO functions and activities (along with the descriptions of each) should provide senior management and project teams an understanding of what PMOs can do for an organization. A provision of the sense of the effort required to implement a PMO can be significant, too. But organizations can approach PMO implementation in steps—and in most cases, they should.

The PMO Competency Continuum

Five general stages of PMO competency levels within an organization are prescribed. These levels are used to assess not only an organization's PMO competency—that is, its ability to integrate a PMO into the organization—but also how well it serves to meet the organization's goals and how efficiently it does it. Exhibit 11-1 describes the PMO competency levels and shows how the PMO would evolve from a very basic one to a center of excellence.

Using Exhibit 11-1, senior management can plan rationally what type and size of PMO will satisfy the organization's immediate goals. Exhibit 11-1 also serves as a road map to evolving into more sophisticated PMOs as their PMO expertise and success grows.

Establishment of a PMO

Establishing a PMO is not easy, but by using Exhibit 11-1, senior management can accomplish the first step—namely, performing an analysis to determine where the organization is and where it needs to go to meet strategic goals. Once the analysis is complete, establishing a PMO should be treated like any other project using a project life cycle—that is, concept, plan, design and build, implement, transition, and maintenance and support. Exhibit 11-2 demon-

Exhibit 11-1. Overview of PMO capabilities across the PMO competency continuum.

Project Oversight	Process Control	Process Support	Business Maturity	Strategic Alignment
Stage 1 **Project Office**	**Stage 2** **Basic PMO**	**Stage 3** **Standard PMO**	**Stage 4** **Advanced PMO**	**Stage 5** **Center of Excellence**
Achieve project deliverables and objectives for cost, schedule, and resource utilization.	Provide a standard and repeatable PM methodology for use across all projects.	Establish capability and infrastructure to support and govern a cohesive project environment.	Apply an integrated and comprehensive project management capability to achieve business objectives.	Manage continuous improvement and cross-department collaboration to achieve strategic business goals.
•1 or more projects •1 project manager	•Multiple projects •Multiple PMs •Program manager •Part-time PMO support staff	•Multiple projects •Multiple PMs •Program managers •Director/Senior program manager •Full-time and part-time PMO staff	•Multiple projects •Multiple PMs •Program managers •PMO director •Dedicated PMO technical and support staff	•Multiple projects •Vice President or Director of Project •Dedicated PMO technical and support staff •Enterprise-wide support staff

Exhibit 11-2. PMO life cycle phases and potential issues.

Concept	Plan	Design and Build	Implement	Transition	Maintenance and Support
Concept phase issues	Plan phase issues	Design/Build phase issues	Implementation phase issues	Transition phase issues	Maintenance and support phase issues
• Establishing a new staff function or department	• Probably require a prototype methodology to design and deliver the PMO	• The model design must be supported	• Management enthusiasm may dwindle	• Defining when the project has ended and the new PMO takes over	• Charge-backs
• The PMO does not generate revenue		• Agreement on the PMO model is a goal	• Organizational culture may resist change		
• PMO's function is primarily oversight	• Probably require using the rolling wave approach	• A life cycle cost model is recommended	• Value of a PMO may be questioned		
• Appears to some that PMO adds more red tape	• Plans will be continuously revised	• Implementation schedule must be realistic	• Manager chosen to lead the PMO may not be the best person for the job		
• A business case may not be clear on the strategic value-added					

strates these phases and the issues likely to be encountered during each phase.

As with any project, designing, developing, and implementing a PMO has a life cycle. Each of the phases in this project will have its own issues that have to be resolved by the project manager. Exhibit 11-2 is self-explanatory, but the issues encountered can be summarized into three: getting buy-in and support from the senior management, overcoming cultural resistance by convincing all stakeholders of the value-added worth from a PMO, and establishing a charge-back process by which every organization contributes its fair share of maintaining the PMO.

Getting buy-in from senior management to implement a PMO is probably not too difficult in most organizations because senior managers typically are open to any suggestion that has the promise of improving the company's ability to accomplish business more efficiently and also adding profitability. The problem is more likely to be in keeping senior managers interested in the PMO so that their support is constant, which means the project manager must constantly communicate with them on a PMO implementation's progress.

Perhaps the most difficult task in implementing a PMO is overcoming the organization's cultural bias—the notion that "we've always done it this way, so why change now." Cultural resistance is more likely to occur in older, more established companies—those that have seen and helped the company grow from a start-up to its current state. To overcome cultural resistance requires a significant amount of emotional intelligence on the part of the project manager and the willingness and patience to communicate with and assure these stakeholders of the value-added worth of the PMO.

One of the major mistakes organizations make when establishing a PMO is to not establish a process for each department to pay its fair share to maintain the PMO. Once the PMO is established, its management, depending on the type and level of PMO, is going to be funded by organizational overhead—that is, those costs that cannot be directly attributable to a specific contract, which would fund the PMO's management and support. So, each division, project, or program that the PMO supports should pay for the PMO's services. This issue becomes particularly important when the PMO is supporting an internal project because external projects can contribute some overhead reimbursement to the project.

Taking a project management approach to implementing the PMO is the only sensible way to establish the PMO, but one additional and very important piece of the PMO establishment puzzle is to understand how it fits into the organization.

PMO Stage Organizations

Each stage of PMO maturity fits into the organization in specific ways. No one organizational structure is any better than another—it depends entirely on what structure works best for the organization—but an understanding of how the PMO fits into a typical structure helps define the type and level of PMO.

This section discusses in some detail the organizational fit of the first three PMO maturity stage organizations. The stage 4 structure is much like that of stage 3 except that its authority and range of activities are much greater. The structure of stage 5 is that of a separate business unit and can look like any other company.

Stage 1 PMO Organization

The stage 1 PMO level of maturity is the most basic level. It can fit anywhere within the organizational structure, but it usually fits under one of the functional groups—for example, there may be a PMO within the engineering group or training group (or both) to support the projects within those groups. Exhibit 11-3 graphically depicts how a stage 1 PMO is organized.

This PMO level is designed to support project managers by giving advice on project tools and techniques, providing policies and procedures, and generally acting as a consultant where they are needed. The PMO typically supports more than one project manager at this level, but there is only one project manager on the PMO staff.

Exhibit 11-3. Stage 1 PMO structure.

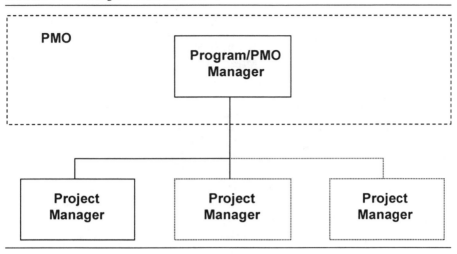

Stage 2 PMO Organization

The stage 2 PMO organization deals with multiple projects and project managers and is managed by a program manager—that is, the head of the PMO serves in the capacity of a program manager with one or more project managers reporting to him or her. There is also a part-time support staff that specializes in things such as finance, risk management monitoring and control, quality, and so on. Exhibit 11-4 depicts this organizational structure.

Whereas the stage 1 PMO easily fits in any organizational structure, the stage 2 PMO organization reports to a higher-level manager so that support across the organization is facilitated—that is, this senior manager acts as the champion (or sponsor) for the PMO and negotiates with other senior management on behalf of the PMO. Exhibit 11-5 depicts how the stage 2 PMO fits into and supports the overall organization.

Note that as the PMO maturity and authority increases, it moves higher into the organization structure.

Stage 3 PMO Organization

The stage 3 PMO organization is also characterized by multiple projects and multiple project managers, but the size, numbers, and

Exhibit 11-4. Stage 2 PMO structure.

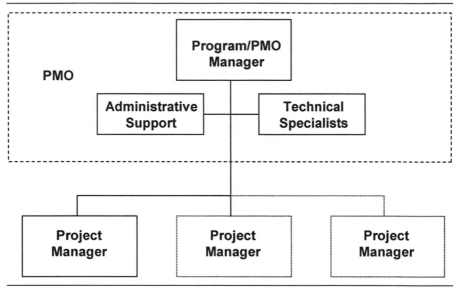

complexity of projects require the PMO to be managed by a director or a senior program manager. Another characteristic of this organization is that it contains both full- and part-time support staff. Exhibit 11-6 shows the stage 3 organization, and Exhibit 11-7 depicts how this type PMO operates across a company's organizational structure.

The first three stages of PMO maturity are sufficient for most small to medium-size companies. Larger companies require additional capability in their PMOs, and megasized global companies evolve their PMOs into a center of excellence.

Stage 4 PMO Organization

Stage 4 PMO organizations are very similar to stage 3 organizations; both have the same basic structure and fit into the company's organizational structure in the same way. The difference is in the size and complexity of the stage 4 PMO. There are both individual project managers as well as program managers, who manage several similar projects, working within the organization. This level of sophistication and complexity requires that the PMO

Exhibit 11-5. Stage 2 PMO in the organizational structure.

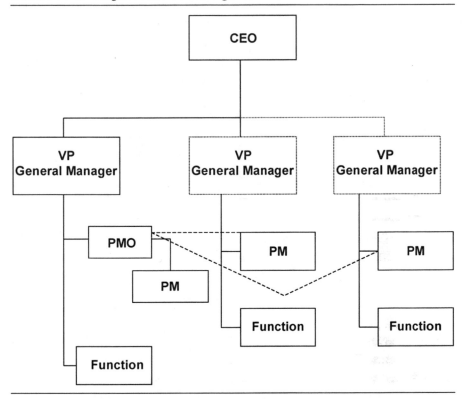

manager be a senior manager—that is, a director-level manager—as opposed to being a senior project manager. This level of PMO maturity also requires a fully dedicated support staff.

Stage 5 PMO Organization

The stage 5 PMO organization is known as the center of excellence and because of its size, authority, and expertise becomes a separate business center. Its organization can be likened to that of project organizational structure. It has its own support staff, the manager is a vice president or general manager, and the center can execute its own contracts, deal with customers and vendors, and generally operate as a separate business. The center of excellence (sometimes referred to as enterprise PMO) has broad authority across

Exhibit 11-6. Stage 3 PMO structure.

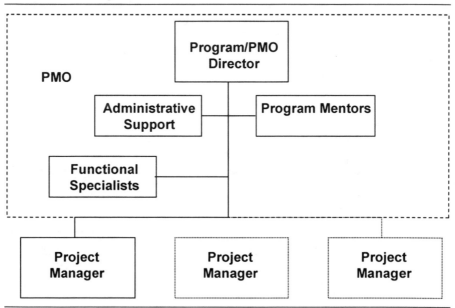

the entire organization because it conducts analyses and examinations of project team structures and their alignment within the relevant organizational group. It is continuous in its efforts to establish the project team and PMO structure and alignment that will maximize capability in the project management environment. A good example of this PMO structure can be found at NASA. As shown in Exhibit 11-8, it is obvious that the PMO oversees and drives all of NASA's projects.

Designing and implementing a PMO takes careful and deliberate consideration of the organization's strategic goals, the type of PMO needed to meet these goals, and how it should be structured to best support the company's business.

Summary

The PMO is a concept that gained support after the failure of so many projects during the early 1990s, particularly in the information technology industry. There are two PMO models that organi-

Exhibit 11-7. Stage 3 PMO in the organizational structure.

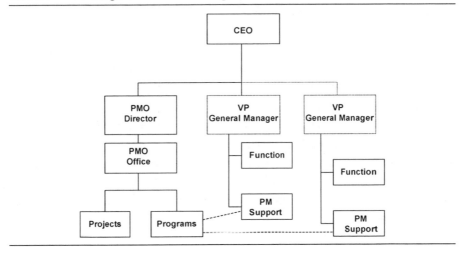

Exhibit 11-8. Stage 5 PMO structure.

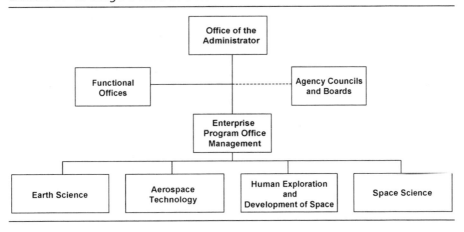

zations use. In small or medium-size companies, PMOs typically are designed to be consultative in nature, and in large—especially global—companies PMOs are centralized. Either model can work in any company. But it is imperative that the company choose the model that best meets its business and strategic goals.

In the consultative model, the PMO provides support and advice to the project manager and his or her team by providing procedures, policies, and technical advice about project management. In the centralized model, the PMO actually runs the projects.

Every organization approaches PMO implementation differently depending on the need and urgency of establishing and using a PMO. There are five levels of maturity an organization can achieve as its PMO evolves, but the first three levels (basic through having a senior project or program manager direct PMO operations) is sufficient for most companies. Larger companies opt to evolve their PMOs to the fourth level, which provides project managers and teams for all company projects. Finally, the fifth level (the center of excellence) is the level that megasized, and especially global, companies use. The center of excellence is designed to be a separate business center that is headed by a very senior vice president or general manager. The center of excellence essentially drives a company's business initiatives.

CHAPTER 12

The Developmental Phase

Make no little plans; they have no magic to stir men's blood.

—DANIEL HUDSON BURNHAM
(1846–1912)
Chief of Columbian Exposition Construction

The developmental phase, sometimes called the planning phase, is where the project is refined and all the preparations for implementing, monitoring, and controlling it are completed. It is also during this phase that the project team membership is determined, and negotiations for these individuals are completed.

The importance of planning cannot be overstated. The conceptual phase is crucial in establishing the bounds of the project and determining the details of exactly what is required as an output of the project, but without a plan to achieve these requirements, the conceptual phase is useless. The activities of the developmental phase operationalize the activities of the conceptual phase. The first step in this process is to finalize the project team's membership.

Establishing the Project Team

During the conceptual phase, one of the first things the project manager does is to form a core project team. This team usually consists of supervisory or senior employees who have broad experience and expertise in the functional areas of the project. They probably will not become part of the operating team—at least not many of them will—because the project team needs to consist of people who will actually do the work of the project or supervise key portions of the project's work. The project engineer, for example, might be a senior technical person whose responsibilities revolve more around ensuring that the technical specifications of the project are met than in actually performing the work of building the project. But generally the core project team is an initial team that helps to define the project and the project team. By the time the project progresses to this phase, the project manager should have determined precisely what types of resources are required—that is, what skill sets are needed and the levels of experience, and the people he or she would like on the team by name.

Many inexperienced project managers are reluctant to approach functional managers with specific names. They usually request support to perform certain technical functions and then rely on the functional manager to provide the talent they need. The problem with this approach is that the managers are not likely to assign their best staff members to the project unless they have a direct interest in it—that is, they are a major stakeholder. Usually, they will keep their best people available for the functional group requirements, or they will assign those who do not happen to have other contracts to work on, in which case they may or may not be the most highly skilled individuals in the group. The point is that project managers need to approach functional managers with specific requests. It may be that the functional manager is unable to accommodate the request because of previous commitments to other projects, but by making specific requests, the project manager will have established the level of expertise and experience needed for the project.

Most organizations use some variation of matrix management. Whether the organization takes on the classical matrix structure or is a traditional structure that supports cross-functional teams, the project manager is faced with a dilemma: He or she does not have functional authority over project personnel and cannot dictate the team membership. The best the project manager can do is to identify whom he or she wants and then negotiate hard to get these people.

Negotiating for Team Members

Project managers must have excellent communication skills and, in particular, excellent negotiation skills. Negotiating for resources is usually a continuing process throughout the project's life cycle because of the constant battle with other functional and project priorities. There are things that the project manager can do, though, that will make the chore of negotiating easier and increase the chances of success.

The best preparation for negotiating for resources is to know the project thoroughly. The project manager should know more about the project—its scope, any contract requirements, technical and personnel requirements, and the final output—than anyone else. Yet many project managers fail in their negotiation attempts because they don't take the next step of organizing and summarizing all their information so that it is succinct, concise, and easily retrievable. The key to negotiating with a functional manager is in being able to talk about the project in a way that clearly:

- Explains the goals and objectives of the project.
- Ties the project goals and objectives to the goals and objectives of the organization.
- Shows how the project will directly benefit the functional group.
- Shows why the project requires very specific skill levels and experience.

These four things can be accomplished only if the project manager is thoroughly familiar with every aspect of the project and has consciously thought through each need and step in the project's life cycle.

The best approach to preparing for negotiations with functional managers is to write a point paper: a short, succinct paper with bulleted points summarizing the project. Actually, this point paper serves two purposes: It is an excellent way to learn all the aspects of the project, and it is a good document to negotiate from with the functional manager. It is usually a good idea to have something in hand to leave with the functional manager as well, and the point paper serves this purpose nicely.

Assigning Project Staff

As the project team takes shape, each member should be assigned to refining the project and specifically to writing the project plan. As we shall see later in this chapter, the completed project plan requires some detailed analyses leading to the development and use of many of the technical tools discussed in Part I. Hence, the project manager needs to staff the project team with skilled and experienced personnel as quickly as possible. Bear in mind that the project manager's role is not to develop the plan unilaterally but rather to be responsible for directing the efforts of the team to do it. Most of the project work, especially in the concept and planning phases, is best done by a team as the result of brainstorming each of the issues.

The ideal project team will be one in which the members are the subject matter experts for the project tasks, have significant experience in analyzing and planning project work, are better-than-average writers, and will be the individuals who will actually do the work once the project is implemented.

Scheduling the Project Kickoff

Every project needs a *kickoff meeting,* the first formal meeting of the project team and stakeholders. Where exactly in the process it should occur is a matter of judgment by the project manager. However, the kickoff meeting should be as early in the process as possible. My preference is to have the meeting near the end of, or as the last activity of, the conceptual phase. Sometimes, though, the kickoff meeting best fits somewhere near the beginning of the development phase because there is a lack of sufficient information to conduct a meaningful kickoff meeting. There are those who argue that a kickoff meeting should not be held until the end of the development phase because not enough is known about the project until all the planning has been completed. The problem with this approach is that too much time elapses, and the real benefits of the kickoff meeting cannot be realized. Holding a kickoff meeting too soon leaves the participants with the feeling that the project is unorganized or lacking in definition. Determining the best time to kick off the project requires a close look at what the kickoff meeting is to accomplish.

The kickoff meeting should be scheduled and chaired by the project manager. A word of caution is important. The kickoff meeting is often viewed as being within the purview of the senior manager of new-business development. It is very difficult to control the meeting when a senior person feels or thinks he or she is in charge of it. Therefore, it is important to establish beforehand whether this type of situation will exist and to try to reach an understanding about what each person's role will be.

Once the roles are established, the kickoff meeting should be scheduled, and all team members and stakeholders should be invited. At this meeting, it is much better to err on the side of inviting too many people than to slight a stakeholder. At a minimum, the kickoff meeting should accomplish the following:

- Introduce the team members and the stakeholders.
- Review the project's scope.
- Review the project's output—that is, the project's purpose.
- Identify potential risks and preliminary plans to mitigate the risks (it is always wise to discuss known risks at the kickoff meeting because it provides a forum to discuss the risks and often results in plans or strategies that will eliminate the risks altogether).
- Present immediate plans for the project, and describe what each project team member will be doing in the next several days.

It is not difficult to see why many project managers are reluctant to schedule a kickoff meeting until they have completed all the planning. The risk of holding such a meeting too soon is that questions may be raised that cannot be answered, resulting in embarrassment for the project manager. Unfortunately, senior management and customers view the kickoff meeting as evidence that the project is moving, and they will want that to occur at the earliest possible time. It is a delicate balance and one that requires judgment and experience from the project manager.

Analyzing the Project Requirements: Preparing to Write the Project Plan

Distinguishing between the conceptual and development phases of the life cycle is difficult because the activities of each are virtually the same. The major difference between the two phases is one of degree of detail. In the conceptual phase, the project manager is concerned with a broad view of the project—that is, the big picture. In the development phase, the project manager is concerned with defining the specific and discrete elements of the big picture.

There are several tasks associated with analyzing and refining the project requirements:

- Understanding customer requirements
- Defining the project objectives
- Defining critical success factors
- Making make-or-buy decisions

Understanding Customer Requirements

If the project manager has diligently evaluated the project requirements during the first phase and verified the evaluation results with the customer, then this step is relatively straightforward. It is simply an opportunity for the project manager to double-check the previous assumptions and conclusions about the project and to fill in any missing details.

Revisiting the customer requirements at this point is necessary also because the project team is now in place. Therefore, this becomes an opportunity for the project manager to ensure that all the project team members have a complete understanding of the project requirements. Reviewing the requirements with the team at this point in the project has the added advantage that the new team members will have a fresh perspective of the project and its requirements. Hence, there will probably be different, and maybe better, interpretations of the customer's needs that will have to be clarified.

Defining the Project Objectives

The project objectives—what the project is to accomplish or its reason for being—have to be completely defined. The objectives in large measure define the technical approach. Unless the objectives are clearly understood, the technical solution will either provide a product that cannot meet the requirements or one whose capability far exceeds the customer's needs (which is termed *goldplating*).

A classic example of the case of exceeding the customer's needs occurred with regularity during the mid-1970s, when the Department of Defense, in response to the fuel crisis, started procuring advanced flight simulators to reduce the amount of actual aircraft flight time needed for training. Those of us who were responsible for writing the specifications for this training equipment felt that the simulators had to duplicate real-world conditions as closely as possible. In our defense, we really didn't know any better at the time, because no real data existed to the contrary. Consequently, the specifications we wrote were very detailed and required engineering tolerances equally as stringent as on the actual aircraft being simulated. In fact, we often lifted whole sections of aircraft specifications and used them verbatim in the simulator specifications. In addition, the visual systems we required were good enough to show discrete branches and leaves on trees, as well as moving vehicles on the ground. These stringent specifications drove the cost of our simulators to the point that a single weapons systems trainer—a six-degree-of-freedom simulator with air-to-air or air-to-ground fighting capability—cost more than the real aircraft. To make matters worse, no one did an analysis before procuring the training equipment to determine what capability was needed in the simulator or how it could be used most efficiently. Instead, it was built with little or no consultation with the user, and then it was left to the user to structure a training program around the equipment. In other words, the training equipment, not the training, was the focus. Happily, the DOD has realized that the training program itself is where the focus belongs, and simulators, along with white boards, overhead projectors, and flip charts, are just training media.

Accurately defined project objectives prior to project implementation, then, are very important.

Defining Critical Success Factors

The project team has to define those factors related to the project that will directly influence whether the project is a success. There are factors—either events happening at particular times or people who have strong interests in the project—that influence whether the project's goals and objectives are met. This is different from the risk assessment, although a critical success factor could also be a risk area. For instance, a critical success factor might be the public support of the project by a senior manager in the organization. However, the senior manager may be withholding support until he or she sees positive results from an upcoming test. On the one hand, it is critical to the success of the project to have this particular manager's support, but there is a risk that he or she might not give it.

Other critical success factors could include the following:

- Improvements to the components being procured for the project
- Availability of personnel with particular skills
- Strong first article test results
- Error-free demonstrations of the prototype
- On-time and on-budget delivery

Some of these factors may be risks as well, but some of them, such as the error-free demonstration, might provide a tremendous boost to the project if it occurs, but might not be more than a temporary disappointment if it does not occur. Defining these critical success factors early helps the team write them into the project plan so that they can work toward making the success factors a reality.

Making Make-or-Buy Decisions

Once the potential problems and the critical success factors are defined, the team is in a position to assess what has to be done against the organization's capability to do it. Often, it becomes clear that some requirements of the project demand an expertise that does not exist in the organization. To cope with this eventuality, you will have essentially three choices:

1. Procure the needed capability from a consultant or from a vendor
2. Team with one or more organizations who do have the capability
3. Hire additional personnel who have the required capability

Generally, the third option is not an option at all for the project manager, although there are circumstances in which the project manager might make such a recommendation and the senior management would agree because that provides a capability that could be used for other projects as well. The most likely scenario would be either the first or the second choice—hence, the term "make or buy." The project manager, along with the project team, has to make the decision about what part or parts of the project the organization will do and what part or parts of the project they will procure from someone else. Notice that it is not entirely a question of whether the organization can do a particular piece of work, but whether the organization will or should do the work. There may be a perfectly good reason that it would be better to procure a piece of work that the organization has in-depth experience and expertise in. The most obvious reason it might be better to procure some of the work from outside the organization is that a smaller company might be able to do the work at a lower cost.

Make-or-buy decisions have tremendous ramifications for a company. Many senior managers will not easily agree to buy a service if the home organization can do it, because it means that there will be less coverage—that is, direct charges to the contract—for the manager's employees. Furthermore, organizations cannot allow a teammate to have such a large percentage of the contract that the teammate becomes the prime contractor. But all that not-withstanding, the project manager, theoretically at least, can make the recommendation to "buy" none, some, or even all of the services and products from outside the organization. Determining what percentage the organization will make and what percentage it will buy is a crucial decision to the planning process.

Writing the Project Plan

The project plan really was begun during the conceptual phase of the project when the scope was defined and high-level budgets, schedules, and resource requirements were estimated. As soon as the project team is established, all the elements of the project plan can be refined, and the plan can be written.

There are five steps in the project planning phase of the project's life cycle. Exhibit 12-1 lists these steps and shows the technical tools that the project team can use to accomplish each of the steps.

Decomposing the Project into Tasks and Subtasks

Decomposing the project into tasks and subtasks is best done through the development of the WBS. The best way to develop a WBS is through brainstorming sessions with the project team, writing each task or subtask on a sticky note and sticking the notes on a wall or white board. Brainstorming reduces the risk of forgetting a task, and sticking the notes on a wall allows the team to consolidate tasks, eliminate duplication, and move the tasks around until

Exhibit 12-1. Project planning steps and planning tools.

Planning Steps	Project Management Tools
Decompose project into tasks and subtasks.	Work breakdown structure.
Determine task durations and interdependencies.	PERT or precedence diagramming charts.
Develop project schedules.	Work breakdown structure Gantt Chart.
Estimate task costs and develop the project budget.	Work breakdown structure.
Determine final resource requirements.	Work breakdown structure Task responsibility matrix.

the team is satisfied with their placement within the WBS hierarchy.

Once the WBS is developed, any of several project management software packages can be used to put the WBS into its final form. Some of the most popular software packages are Microsoft Project, TimeLine, Primavera, Project Scheduler, Borland Star Team Enterprise Advantage, Corel iGrafx Process 2003 for Six Sigma, and SureTrak. All of these software packages will display and print the WBS in the indentured format. However, not all will display and print it in the graphical format.

Determining Task Durations and Interdependencies

Once the WBS is developed, all the other planning tools can be developed too. The next one needed is the precedence diagram (PD) (or PERT, as appropriate). The PD is used to show the interdependencies of the tasks and subtasks. It is necessary to construct the PD because it is only after the network is analyzed that the next step, developing the schedule, can be accomplished. The network logic shows how the tasks relate to each other and which ones can be done in parallel. The network also defines the overall schedule duration.

The PD is developed by first determining how long each individual task and subtask takes. The project manager, or the designated lead person for a specific project area, determines how long the tasks and subtasks take by talking with the individuals who will be doing the work. During the process of determining how long the task takes, the project team should also determine how the task relates to other tasks.

Generally, the responsible individual will be able to estimate with great accuracy how long the work will take because that person has performed the same or similar tasks many times before. This individual also knows what information is required from other tasks before the task can start. Occasionally, the work will be completely new, or the task will involve significant research and development so that estimating the time accurately is difficult. In those cases, the project manager, along with the appropriate subject matter experts, will use the PERT analysis technique to determine the schedule.

Constructing the PD network also serves other purposes, but because of the importance of the network analysis and the critical information derived from the analysis, particularly for planning, it is worth repeating what kinds of information can be derived from the analysis:

- Schedule length
- Critical path (the longest path in the network and the path that has the least slack in its activities)
- Total slack in the project and slack by individual task
- A graphical view of how each task relates to every other task

With the network analysis complete, the project team can develop the project schedules.

Developing Project Schedules

An excellent tool for developing and portraying schedules is the Gantt chart, developed around 1917 by Henry Gantt, a pioneer in scientific management. The Gantt chart is, in its basic form, a

schedule chart depicting the project tasks and their associated beginning and ending dates. Usually, these dates are connected by a
solid bar to graphically portray the task's duration. Exhibit 12-2
is an example of a Gantt chart showing a schedule for designing,
developing, purchasing, and installing a management information
system.

Most projects, particularly long and complex ones, require several different schedules. For instance, you as the project manager
will always want to have a master schedule to show the major
tasks and the overall beginning and ending dates. In addition,
there may be a requirement for additional schedules that show
special events—for instance, tests. A common use of the Gantt
chart is to show scheduled meetings or report due dates. Sometimes the project is so complex that several Gantt charts are
needed to show the project detail.

Estimating Task Costs and Determining a Project Budget

The task costs are determined in the same way that the task durations are determined: The project team members talk to the individuals who will be doing the work. These individuals will have a
good sense of how much the task will cost. If, for instance, the task
requires only labor and no equipment or materials, the cost for it
will be the labor rate of the individual(s) doing the task times the
number of hours required to do the task.

Once the individual tasks have a cost against them, it is an easy
matter to aggregate the costs of all the tasks under major WBS
headings and finally for the total project.

Whether determining a project budget is required is a matter
of some controversy. Some people argue that this is a waste of time
when the budget is dictated by the organization. Clearly, this step
is necessary when the planning is being done in preparation for
submitting a bid for a contract to do a project. In that case, the
budget development determines the cost and is the basis for the
bid price. But what about when the project manager is given
the project and told what the budget is? Is there any reason why
the project manager should redetermine the budget? The answer
is a resounding yes!

Exhibit 12-2. *Typical Gantt chart.*

Gantt Chart for Management Information System

ID	Task Name	Duration	August	September	October	November	December
1	Assess Requirements	14 days					
2	Design Management Information System	21 days					
3	Develop Hardware/Off-the-Shelf Software Parts List	7 days?					
4	Purchase Hardware/Software	7 days					
5	Integrate Hardware/Software	7 days					
6	Test Computer Terminals	2 days?					
7	Install LAN Lines	14 days					
8	Connect Terminals to LAN System	3 days?					
9	Develop MIS Software	21 days					
10	Test MIS Software	7 days					
11	Test MIS System	14 days					

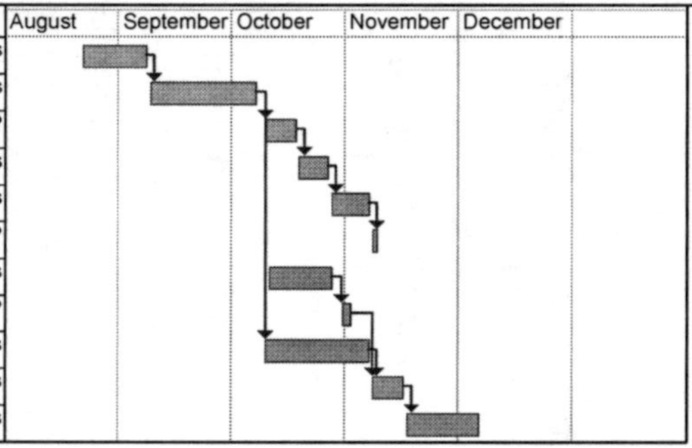

When a project manager is handed a budget to do a project, the budget is usually the result of either a top-level estimate developed when the project was in the very early stage of conceptualization or a contract won through a competitive bid. Either way, the chances are that the budget is not realistic.

Consider the case of the contract from a competitive bid. The contract was probably awarded because the organization had the lowest bid—too often far less than it really takes to do the work. Not only that, but senior management always reduces the contract price by the profit amount and often reduces it further to provide a reserve. In either case, the project manager is almost always starting the project with, at best, a very tight budget, or, at worse, a completely unachievable one. Therefore, the project manager has to develop an accurate budget to know at the beginning whether there are likely to be any budget problems. It is possible to accomplish the project within budget by reassessing the skill requirements, type and quality of equipment and materials, and number of personnel needed to do the job. However, this replanning can only be achieved if the amount of the potential shortfall is known.

Determining the Resources for a Project

The project team will have determined, with a high degree of accuracy, the resource requirements for the project. However, it is only after the WBS is fully developed and each task and subtask is identified that the team will really know what resources are going to be required. Once this is done, the project manager can adjust the team membership if required.

It is also at this time that the project manager can assign specific duties to the team members, because the tasks can be completely identified and defined. A tool that helps in assigning these tasks and helps the project manager track and control the project is a task responsibility matrix, shown in Exhibit 12-3. This matrix is designed to show who is responsible for accomplishing the work of each task in the WBS. In addition, it usually shows how long the task will take, and it can also show what budget is assigned to the

Exhibit 12-3. Task responsibility matrix.

Task Responsibility Matrix				
Project Manager _____ Project Name/Number _____				
Project Sponsor _____ Project Customer Organization _____				
WBS Number	WBS Description	Task Duration	Primary Person Responsible	Secondary Person Responsible

task. This becomes particularly helpful when the budget, actual expenditures, and the earned value numbers are collected for project tracking.

Developing the Project Plan Format

Exhibit 12-4 is a generic format for a project plan. With this format, a project team can develop a plan that can be used to successfully accomplish a project's goals and objectives. This format is generic because it has been developed over a number of years and represents the basic elements that are required in nearly any project. Many organizations or customers have developed their own plan formats to accommodate special requirements of the project. Therefore, the wise project manager will determine, during the conceptual phase, whether there are special plan requirements or not. If not, the format of Exhibit 12-4 will serve most situations.

Creating the Executive Summary

This section is always written last because it is only after all the details of the project are known that the project manager and team can summarize the project.

Exhibit 12-4. A generic project plan format.

I. Executive Summary

II. Project Requirements and Objectives

III. General Methodology of Technical Approach

IV. Contractual Requirements

V. Schedules

VI. Resource Requirements
A. Equipment
B. Materials
C. People

VII. Potential Risks

VIII. Performance Evaluation

The executive summary, typically directed to senior management, provides a summary of the background, scope, and objectives of the project. It should also contain a brief overview of how the project will be accomplished, identify the customers, and talk about any special problems expected in the project and how they will be handled. For instance, if the project is large enough or complex enough that team members and consultants are needed, then it should be discussed in general terms. Risks and strategies for risk mitigation should also be addressed.

The executive summary should be viewed as exactly that—a summary. It usually is relatively short, about two pages, but can be longer depending on the size and complexity of the project. It should be written as succinctly as possible so that readers can quickly read and digest it but still be able to talk about the project with authority.

Determining Project Requirements and Objectives

This section goes into depth about what the project is all about. It clearly states exactly what the requirements of the project are, the objectives of the project, the scope (that is, how large the project is), how long it will take to accomplish, how many and what type of end products, what the measure of success will be, and how the project goals mesh with the organization's goals. This section is very detailed and can be several pages long.

Choosing General Methodology or Technical Approach

This section provides a narrative description of how the project manager and team will accomplish the project's goals. It should describe both the managerial and the technical approaches to accomplishing the project. Precise details of how to manufacture a part or the steps in developing some software are not required, but the general processes of each step of the project should be described.

This section should also discuss the relationship of the project's technical approach to existing technologies. If it is anticipated that new and different technologies will be required, this section should discuss how they will be integrated into the project.

Determining Contractual Requirements

This section describes any special contractual requirements relative to the project: special reporting or deliverable schedules, payment cycles, specific types and numbers of tests and product demonstrations, reporting formats, required meetings or project reviews, and place and time of final delivery of the product.

This section also documents any special contractual requirements on vendors or consultants to the organization.

If the project customer is internal to the organization and there are no vendors or consultants involved with it, this section is not needed.

Creating Schedules

The schedule section of the project plan may be quite long, and the schedules themselves may need to be drawn on fold-out sheets to accommodate them. The best approach is to provide a summary of key schedule points within the body of the plan and to attach the schedules themselves as appendixes to the plan. That way, the appendixes can be detached if necessary, eliminating the problem of reading fold-out sheets in the middle of the plan document.

There may be more than one schedule in any project. There can be as many as five or six schedules for even relatively short and uncomplicated projects. How many schedules to prepare is strictly a function of the customer requirements (sometimes a customer will dictate separate schedules for different events) or whether preparing additional schedules will clarify or simplify the project tracking. How many schedules is usually a judgment call by the project manager. The key is to prepare as many schedules as you need to track the project.

Determining Resource Requirements

Resources include all the personnel, equipment, facilities, and materials needed to accomplish the requirements of the project. It is better to break out these different resources to track their costs. Personnel, for instance, represent pure labor costs; materials is a cost category of its own.

All resources needed for the project are tabulated here. There are several reasons that a detailed accounting of all resources is important in the project plan. First, it is the only way to truly identify the project cost. Second, it provides the project manager with the leverage to negotiate for the needed resources. Third, once the project cost is determined, if the budget is less than the costs, the project manager and team can determine where cost reductions might be made by reassessing the project requirements against the identified resources.

Identifying Potential Risks

This is one of the most important sections of the project plan. It is the responsibility of the project manager and team to identify as many potential problem areas or risks as possible. The project sponsor or customer is also responsible for identifying any known risks. The reason is simple: It is far better to plan for a problem than to be surprised by it and have to work around it.

There are generally three types of risks: knowns, known unknowns, and unknown unknowns. A *known risk* is one that the project manager knows could and probably will happen, and the impact is known—for example, some data or product is needed from one project before the second project can begin. If the schedule is so tight between the two that any delay in the first project would cause a delay in the second, then this is a known risk. A *known unknown* type of risk is one in which the project manager knows something will go wrong but does not know what the impact will be. For instance, we know that we will be receiving a telephone bill but don't know what the charges will be. An *unknown unknown* is one in which it is not known what will happen, nor is it known what the impact will be.

Clearly, the project team cannot anticipate every problem. However, using historical data and the experience of the team members, the project manager can plan for most of the risk. For risks that cannot be anticipated, management reserves or other contingency plans can be developed.

Determining Performance Evaluation

The last part of the plan format is the performance evaluation section. It is absolutely crucial for the project team to determine how the work of the project will be measured and the performance evaluated. Otherwise, how will the project manager know if the requirements of the project are met?

Often, projects have associated with them standards that are required by the customer, government regulating agencies, or other coding organizations. If that is the case, the evaluation procedures may be straightforward and clear. However, if there are no such existing standards, the project manager and the project team must determine how they are going to assess the project's progress and what kind of "goodness" measure they will use. This evaluation strategy will have to be acceptable to the customer, and the project plan is an ideal way to communicate the strategy to all the stakeholders, including the customer.

Reviewing the Project Plan with the Customer

Finally, the project plan has to be reviewed with the customer regardless of whether the customer is internal or external to the organization. If the project is the result of winning a competitive bid, the project plan is a part of the proposal that the organization has to submit in response to the customer's request for proposal. When the winner of a competitive bid is selected and the contract is awarded, the winner's proposal becomes a part of the contract. In this case, the project plan has been reviewed and approved by the customer. In the case of an internal customer, however, it becomes the responsibility of the project manager to schedule time with the appropriate customer representatives to review and explain the project plan.

The need to review the project plan at this stage is simple: The next step is to implement the project and begin work. This is the last opportunity the customer will have to review the project prior to starting work. It is also the last opportunity, prior to starting work, the project manager will have to ensure that the project team has correctly captured the customer's intent and accurately interpreted the project's objectives and requirements.

Summary

The development or planning phase of the project is where the project is operationalized. All the analyses come together in a plan that allows the project manager to monitor and control the project to a successful conclusion. Some of the major tools used in the analyses of this phase are the:

- WBS
- PERT or precedence diagram (PD)
- Gantt charts
- Task responsibility matrix
- Project plan format

One of the key responsibilities for the project manager during this phase is to review the project plan with the customer. This review is the last action taken in this phase and is the final step toward implementing the project. Therefore, the review is the last opportunity for the customer to ensure that the project is going in the desired direction, and it is the last opportunity for the project manager to ensure that his or her interpretation of the project's objectives and requirements is the same as the customer's.

Once the project plan has final approval, the project can be implemented.

CHAPTER 13

The Implementation Phase

Hold fast the time! Guard it, watch over it, every hour, every minute! Unregarded it slips away, like a lizard, smooth, slippery, faithless, a pixy wife.

—THOMAS MANN
The Beloved Returns

The term *implementation phase* may be a little misleading because it implies simply putting something into motion. The implementation phase is indeed that, but it is much, much more. It is often called the main phase of the project—the phase during which the actual work is performed. Consequently, this is the phase in which the project is started, monitored, and controlled.

Project implementation is the process of putting the project plan into action. The project plan is the road map of how the project should progress; the implementation phase is where the plan is turned into reality.

Monitoring is the process of assessing project performance or how the project is doing against what was planned. Very quickly it will become apparent to the project manager and team just how well they have planned the project when they start measuring actual against estimated performance.

Project control is the process of controlling the deviations from the plan. During the planning phase, key things such as the project budget and schedule are determined. Controlling the project's progress means controlling how closely the actual expenditures and work accomplished adhere to the plan.

Implementing the Project

Once a project is approved and given the go-ahead, the project manager's next step is to put those things in motion required to start performing the work of the project. There are several steps that the project manager and the parent organization must go through to ensure that the project gets started on the right foot and moves according to the plan. Exhibit 13-1 shows the key steps in this process. These steps are planned during the development phase, but obviously cannot be acted on until the project manager and team receive the final approval to proceed. Note that many of the steps in Exhibit 13-1 are not sequential. They can be started in parallel. The primary consideration at this stage is to get the project under way as soon as possible while ensuring that each of the critical steps are accomplished.

Set Up Cost Accounts

On small projects, it is generally not too difficult to monitor and control the project from one simple budget. The budget is used to

Exhibit 13-1. Steps in implementing a project.

PROJECT IMPLEMENTATION PROCESS

1. Set up cost accounts.
2. Refurbish/rent/buy facilities.
3. Collocate team.
4. Design a monitoring system.
5. Issue work orders.
6. Contract with vendors.
7. Issue Request for Proposal (RFP) for competitive bids.
8. Hire personnel.
9. Train personnel.

track the project as a whole, and usually there is no compelling requirement to track the budget in greater detail than, say, the third level of the WBS. In larger, more complex projects, this approach would not have enough sensitivity to the nuances in performance that occur in multiple tasks or subtasks. Consequently, tracking the project variances would be impossible. Specifically, project overruns could be detected but not the source of the overrun.

To overcome this problem, the concept of *cost accounts* was developed: breaking the project down into small elements and monitoring each of these elements individually. Each element has its own cost or budget associated with it so that its progress can be measured directly against the planned budget.

In Chapter 5, we discussed the WBS and the work package in detail. The work package is described by a WBS dictionary. The term *dictionary* is used because it defines exactly what and how the work will be accomplished. The WBS dictionary for each work package provides the following information:

- A short but concise description of the work to be accomplished
- A schedule to begin and finish the work
- Who, by name, is responsible for accomplishing the work
- A list of labor resources, materials, and equipment needed to accomplish the task
- A budget for the task

All of these characteristics of the work package are elements of the cost account with the exception that, in a cost account, the budget has to be time-phased to be monitored. The budget for each individual task can be time-phased on a Gantt chart or on one of the spreadsheets, such as Microsoft Excel, allowing a day-by-day assessment of expenditures against the plan.

Refurbish/Rent/Buy Facilities

Project managers usually do not have to be concerned with preparing or buying new facilities, but it can happen. Some projects require special work spaces or specialized tools, test equipment, or environmentally controlled work spaces. Under any of these circumstances, the project manager might find him- or herself running a construction or refurbishment project before the primary project can begin.

Collocate the Project Team

It is strongly recommended that the project team be collocated if at all possible. This does not mean that the team has to be in the same large room, but all the members should be on the same floor of the building and, ideally, in the same general section on the floor.

There are several reasons why collocating the team is beneficial:

- It enhances good communication between the project manager and the team and among the team members.
- Working closely together on a project builds team spirit.
- Team morale is enhanced when team members feel that they are physically and mentally connected.
- Project problems often can be avoided when team members are close enough to discuss difficulties as they occur.

Although the ideal situation is for the team to be collocated, the reality is that most organizations do not have the space to collocate each project team. The next best alternative is to establish a "war room" for the team: a room set aside for the exclusive use of the project team. This is a large enough room for team meetings and for maintaining files relevant to the project.

Design a Monitoring System

Setting up a monitoring system is crucial to the control process. Without a way to track and analyze each of the tasks of a project, it is not possible to make the decisions necessary for controlling the project's progress.

Issue Work Orders

In order for the project to begin, the project manager must issue the appropriate work orders. In addition to authorizing the work to begin, each work order is a small but crucial part of the control process also. The work order specifies how requirements are to be fulfilled, how much can be spent on the task, and how long the work should take. John Nicholas, professor of engineering management at Loyola University, lists the following minimum information that is a part of every work order:[1]

- Statement of work
- Time-phased budget of direct labor hours, materials, and other direct costs
- Schedules, milestones, and relationships to other work packages
- Position of the task in the WBS
- Specifications and requirements
- Cost account number and position in the cost account structure
- Signatures of person authorizing and person accepting responsibility

Contract with Vendors

There are very few projects that do not have some vendor-required items. Although most organizations have a procurement department that specializes in contracting with vendors, it remains the project manager's responsibility to initiate the request for purchase. It is also the project manager, or the designated technical representative, who provides the requisite specifications for the requested item. In some cases, though, in particular when the technical solution requires the services of a team member rather than the services of a vendor, the project manager is responsible for negotiating the teaming agreement.

Issue Request for Proposal for Competitive Bids

The request for proposal (RFP) formally invites contractors or vendors to bid on some part of a project. For instance, your project might require a specialized software program that your company cannot develop. You would then prepare an RFP describing your project's requirement and a detailed specification that qualified companies could bid on. RFPs are issued with precise instructions about how, where, and when bidders should respond. The response to the RFP is a proposal that contains, at a minimum, price and schedule estimates. A proposal also can contain a description of the responder's company, how they manage their tasks, risks associated with task development, and so on, depending on what is specified in the RFP.

For most projects, RFPs to vendors or other contractors are simple one- to five-page documents. Even so, the tendency is to bypass the formal RFP process, and simply call a favored supplier. Resist the urge to bypass the RFP process, because issuing a formal RFP, if only in letter form, provides an audit trail, and it will reduce project costs through competition.

Hire Personnel

In many projects, the organizational strategy is to hire personnel to fill the specialized billets in the project organization. Although the human resources department is responsible for advertising for people and administering the hiring procedures, the project manager generally has the final say on who is hired for the project. Hence, the project manager needs to have a good understanding of interviewing techniques and procedures, as well as a thorough knowledge of the administrative processes, company benefits, and career potential with the organization.

Train Personnel

There may be a requirement to train some project people before they can begin working on the project. For instance, if the project is to develop some specialized software using the customer's processes, procedures, or computer language, it may be necessary for the project manager to develop and schedule some special training courses. Or it may be that the parent organization possesses a cadre of trained personnel but not enough staff for the project. In any event, the project manager is responsible for ensuring that the project team is prepared to accomplish the project's goals and objectives, and that often means a requirement for special training.

Monitoring the Project

Three activities make up the monitoring process: data collecting, data analyzing, and information reporting. The project manager's responsibility is to establish a process for collecting the data—how it will be collected and how often—and set up a reporting hierarchy for disseminating the information after it is analyzed. To a large degree, the reporting hierarchy will already be set as a part of the stakeholder analysis done in the conceptual phase. However, once the project gets under way, people who have not previously shown any interest in the project emerge. A good way to ensure that the reporting hierarchy is correct and is approved is to prepare a reporting matrix like the one in Exhibit 13-2. The wise project manager will then distribute the proposed data distribution format with a memorandum asking for suggested additions and deletions to the reporting chain.

Data Collection

Sources of data are varied, and the project manager must take advantage of every one of them. The average project manager will spend approximately 90 percent of his or her time communicating with the project team, senior management, the customer, and other stakeholders. The majority of this time is spent either collecting or transmitting data.

Sources for data collection include:

- Project status meetings
- Individual task leader reports
- Employee time sheets

Exhibit 13-2. Sample reporting matrix.

Data Item	Report Description	Project Manager	Senior Manager	Director of Software Development	Director of Contracts	Director of Finance	Customer Project Manager	
1	Status reports (monthly)	x	x	x	x		x	
2	Status reports (weekly)	x						
3	Monthly financial reports	x	x			x		
4	Configuration change reports	x		x				
5	Manpower utilization reports	x		x				
6	Exception reports	x	x					
7	Variance reports	x	x				x	
8								
9								
10								

- Vendor and consultant invoices
- Telephone calls
- E-mail
- Management by walking around

Data collection does not have to follow a formal process. In fact, most project data are gathered informally. However, data going out of the project office are most often presented formally through a status report or status briefing.

Data Analysis

Collecting data is only half of the challenge; analyzing it is the second half. We all know what it is like to experience information overload. Because the project manager spends so much time communicating with the project team, often he or she is provided with so much information that it is not possible to process it all. You will quickly learn to distinguish between meaningful and useless data. But to do so requires close attention to detail and the ability to interpret the raw information.

Analyzing the data is a necessary step in the process because data alone do not show its impact on the project. Before any information is processed out of the project team, there has to be an accurate assessment of the impact and a proposed solution for correcting any problems that might exist.

Most project data of concern involve the budget, the schedule, or the performance or quality of the project. Among the tools for analyzing the data relative to these three project characteristics, earned value is being used more and more for analyzing budget and schedule impacts. (Refer to Chapter 7 for a detailed discussion of earned value and how to apply it.)

Many organizations, though, still use a plot of budget against actual expenditures and estimated schedule against actual schedule to analyze progress. An example is shown in Exhibit 13-3 depicting the status of a project's actual expenditures against the budget at the three-month milestone.

The problem with this approach is that the project appears to be over budget but in actuality it may not be. It is not possible to tell from the information available. Suppose, for example, that the project plan called for buying several computers at month 4, but the vendor called to say that she was moving her store to larger quarters and wanted to reduce the size of her inventory before the move. If she offered a reduced price to purchase the computers early, then the actual expenditures would show a marked increase at month 3, but in fact the project would not be over budget. With everything else being equal, the project would actually be under budget. It was precisely this kind of problem that led to the development of the earned value method for accounting for changes in the project's schedule and accurately showing the status of the project.

Another way of analyzing the impact of data on a project is to use a variance worksheet. An example of one is shown in Exhibit 13-4. The variance worksheet is a good tool because it shows the variance in both the budget and the schedule, and, consequently, would suggest that a change in one has a relationship to the other.

Exhibit 13-3. Project budgeted against actual expenditures.

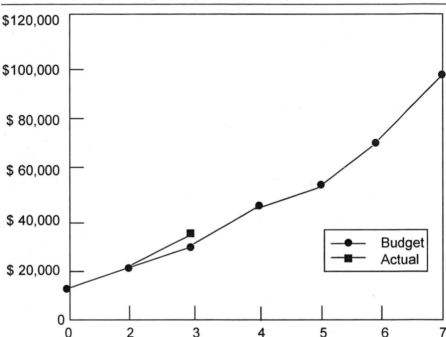

Unfortunately, budget and schedule are not explicitly related on the variance worksheet as they are in the earned value analysis. Therefore, some interpretation is required.

A common use of the variance worksheet is in status reports. Senior managers do not have the time to read long reports, and a variance worksheet provides a lot of information quickly about the project's progress.

Information Reporting

Information reporting is done either through formal reports, such as status reports, or through informational briefings. The project manager or project team uses several different types of reports. All these reports can be classified as status reports in a broad sense, but generally we use the term *status report* to refer to those that routinely describe the project's progress. Other types of reports

Exhibit 13-4. Variance work sheet.

Project Steps	Costs (dollars)			Schedule (days/weeks/months)			
	Budget	Actual	Variance	Total	Planned	Actual	Variance	Budget

detail problems or provide specialized information such as financial deviations or changes to the project's baseline.

Status Reports

A status report is a narrative description of the project's progress, usually provided to senior management and the customer representative on a regular basis, for example, each month. The frequency of the status report, or any other report, usually is a function of how complex or risky the project is. For instance, a project involving new technology with significant financial consequences for the contractor or the customer would likely require frequent, informal status reporting—even daily—and formal reports due weekly or biweekly.

The type of information required on a status report varies from organization to organization. The basic information required on a status report is shown in Exhibit 13-5. Some organizations opt for more detailed status reports rather than having several different reports for specialized reasons.

Variance Reports

Variances are deviations from the planned budget or schedule. Many customers, particularly external customers, require variance reports. The typical variance report has a line graph showing the cumulative budget and schedule plotted against the actual budget and schedule. Any variances—positive if below budget or ahead of schedule, and negative if over budget and behind schedule—have to be explained. If the project is over budget or behind schedule, the variance report will also have to reflect the plans to correct the problems.

Exception Reports

Exception reporting is a part of *exception management*: a way for senior managers to involve themselves in a project when something out of the ordinary happens. For instance, the project manager's functional supervisor, or another senior executive, may impose some limit on a key project element, usually budget, above or below which he or she needs to be informed. An example might

Exhibit 13-5. Sample status report.

STATUS REPORT

Project Name: Report Date:

Project Phase: Report Period:

Project Manager:

Summary of Progress for Period:

Problems Encountered and Action Taken:

Planned Activities for Next Reporting Period:

Anticipated Problems:

Recommendations:

be that as long as actual expenditures are within, say, 10 percent of the budget, the project manager is responsible for correcting the variances. If the budget should exceed the 10 percent limit, above or below, then the project manager is obligated to issue an exception report to the appropriate manager for action.

Incidentally, we automatically assume that below budget or ahead of schedule is a good thing. However, the wise project manager will look with a jaundiced eye at a significant below-budget or ahead-of-schedule report. Why? Being significantly below budget or ahead of schedule might indicate that all the required work on a task is not accomplished.

Controlling the Project

To control a project generally means controlling four things:

1. Cost variances
2. Schedule variances
3. Scope changes
4. Risk

Cost Variances

Cost variances are deviations of actual expenditures from the project budget. Variances occur in every project because it is virtually impossible to predict with 100 percent accuracy what will happen once the project is under way. But controlling these deviations from the budget is a major problem in most projects.

The primary reason budgets are overrun is that the project started with an unreasonable or underestimated budget. We have all heard or read about the horrendous budget overruns that often occur in Department of Defense contracts. For those who are not familiar with the DOD process, the tendency is to assume that the problem of overruns is caused by greedy contractors. Although some of these overruns may be the result of crafty contractors working the system to their benefit, the simple fact is that cost overruns are usually the result of shaving the project costs too much in order to be the lowest bidder in a competitive environment. In every RFP issued by the DOD is a statement to potential contractors declaring that the government has the right to award the contract on other than a cost basis. The RFP usually goes further and states that the contract will be awarded on the basis of *best value*: The highest bidder could win the contract if the government determines that, in the long run, the product from that contractor would be of greater value to the government than any of the other proposed solutions. For instance, one contractor's product might cost significantly more initially than another but cost far less to maintain over the product's lifetime. The best value in this case would be for the government to spend more money initially to get the product whose lifetime or life cycle costs are less. Unfortunately, the government's acquisition process is administered in such a way that by the end of the proposal evaluation cycle, all the competitors will have had their proposals technically leveled; that is, all the competitors will have essentially equal technical solutions, and so the only discriminator left is price. Hence, the "best value" then becomes the lowest price. All too often, the winner will have lowered the bid price so much that the project cannot be accomplished for the contracted amount.

Of course, the lowest bid does not necessarily mean there will be a cost overrun. It certainly is possible to be the low bidder and still have a budget that is sufficient to accomplish the project's goals and objectives. However, what are the consequences of a too-low bid or one that "buys in"? We have already talked about the cost overruns, and, perhaps, convincing the customer to pay for these overruns. Without a renegotiated contract, the only other options for the contractor is to default—that is, have the contract terminated because of the inability to perform—or to perform the contract within the budget provided but at a significantly reduced standard of quality.

The relevance of all this for the average project manager is that whether bidding on a contract or issuing RFPs to prospective vendors, the project manager must be sensitive to the problem of bids that are too low. Inevitably there will be cost overruns or products and services that fall far below the expected quality level.

Low bids are not the only reason for cost overruns. A major problem in many companies is the lack of a budget estimating system or, if there is one, an inaccurate system. There are three types of estimating methods:

1. *Order of Magnitude Estimate.* The order of magnitude estimate is simply a best guess. This type of estimate is usually done to get a ballpark number—a sense of the financial size of a potential project. This type of estimate is made with little or no data to support it. It is based purely on the person's experience and knowledge of the cost to accomplish generally similar projects. The accuracy of this type of estimate is between -50 percent and +100 percent.

2. *Budget Estimate.* The budget estimate is more accurate than the order of magnitude type: approximately -10 percent to +25 percent. An example of the budget-type estimate is the top-down estimate, meaning the estimate is performed by estimating the costs of major tasks or subcomponents of the project and is usually accomplished early in the project's life. These data are based on historical data from similar projects. The top-down method is not a bad estimating method, particularly when done by very experienced people who can draw on a good historical base. But it should be used to aid in the concept phase and refined by a definitive estimate in the development or planning phase.

3. *The Definitive Estimate.* The bottom-up estimate is an example of a definitive estimate. *Bottom-up* means that the estimating process is started at the lowest level of the WBS and aggregated upward to account for every element of the project. This is the most accurate method of the three types. It is accurate to within -10 percent to +15 percent and is done after the WBS has been fully developed.

Notice that in every case, the accuracy ranges of the estimating types are biased toward the positive side of the accuracy ranges. In other words, for the order of magnitude type, the mean of the accuracy range is +75 percent; for the budget-type estimate the mean is +17.5 percent; for the definitive, it is +12.5 percent. What this means is that even with very accurate estimates, the tendency is to underestimate the cost of the project. Hence, the risk of a cost overrun is always present, and cost variances have to be monitored very closely, and managed very tightly.

Schedule Variances

Schedule variances occur usually because of unreasonable schedule constraints. Generally, the project team can estimate the actual duration requirements with reasonable accuracy; and if not, the PERT method provides a means for determining a reasonable task duration. The problem is not so much an inability to estimate the schedule but rather the imposition of a schedule that is too tight.

Most projects are initiated to meet specific needs, such as meeting critical training, the improvement of existing systems, or competitive challenges. In most cases, these projects are reactive responses to a requirement and therefore start later than they should. If the projects are responding to critical needs, there is always a sense of urgency, causing the completion date to be set unreasonably early. The late start and early completion create a compressed schedule that is almost never achievable.

If the cost or schedule variances become too large, the project plan will have to be rewritten, the schedule revised, or the end-item product redesigned.

Scope Changes

Changes to the project baseline are inevitable. They are caused by several different factors, including inaccurate budget and schedule estimates; government health, safety, or environmental standards mandates; and customer or project team recommended changes as project knowledge grows. Change in a project is controlled through a *configuration management process,* a formal process designed by the project manager and team, or in some cases, an in-place organizational process, to screen recommended changes, track approved changes, and update the development process.

1. *Screening Recommended Changes.* Changes to a project can come from the customer as well as from team members and other functional groups. These recommendations should be directed to the project manager, who will assess the impact of the changes to the project. Many organizations have a change control board (CCB) concept to deal with this kind of change. CCBs are routinely found in engineering organizations where project changes have significant technical impact. Membership on a CCB consists of three to five persons representative of the company's technical expertise. CCB meetings are usually scheduled or called rather regularly, since project changes require quick decisions, and waiting for the next CCB meeting could affect the project schedule. If a CCB does not exist, the project manager should form one, because every project, especially complex ones, will have a large number of requests that need to be handled expeditiously. Some of the requested changes will have no effect on the project's budget, schedule, or resources, and the project manager usually is authorized to approve these changes unilaterally. However, if there is an impact on the project, the changes should be approved only by a higher authority or a CCB.

2. *Tracking Approved Changes.* Once a change is approved, the project manager's designated configuration management specialist must document the changes and update the project specifications. In large contracts, the configuration management process is very elaborate and detailed, with each change documented, numbered with a configuration item number, and logged. The configuration management position is so important that it has become a separate labor category and is considered to be a specialist function.

3. *Updating the Development Process.* After the change is approved and the files are updated, the project baseline is updated, the changes are published, and all stakeholders are informed of the changes.

Changes to the baseline often—in fact usually—require a change to the contract. No project changes should ever be approved without an attendant change to the contract. Even if the customer decides to change the baseline configuration and it is determined that there is no impact to the budget or schedule, a no-cost contract modification should be requested by the project manager. Usually the customer will automatically issue one, but the experienced project manager will always insist on having the modification prior to instituting the changes. These contract modifications are necessary because one of the actions at project completion is to determine whether the goals, objectives, and specifications have been met. Without a contract modification, there is no way to track whether or why a change was made.

Risk

The life of a project manager is a life of conflict. In truth, project management is conflict management. The project manager's job is to smoothly negotiate the obstacles encountered during every phase of the project's life. If there were no risk or conflict in a project, there would be no need for a project manager—project management would become an administrative task. But risk is two-sided; there is the possibility of loss and the potential for gain. Project risks can exhibit extremes of both sides—the losses are great if the risk event occurs unabated, but the gains can be immense if the risk is planned for and eliminated or at least mitigated and made manageable.

Risk Defined

Risk is characterized by three components:

1. *The event*—that is, what can happen to the project, good or bad?
2. *The probability of event occurrence*—that is, what are the chances the event will happen?
3. *The impact to the project*—that is, what is the effect on the project, good or bad, if the event actually does occur?

Types of Risk

There are two types of risks: business and pure, or insurable, risk. Risk is not necessarily negative; it may be an opportunity for gain.

The key to risk management is recognizing the potential risk events and whether they can be directed and controlled for a neutral or positive effect on the project. If the risk event can only lead to negative impacts, then it should not be attempted; it should be avoided or transferred to someone else or to another organization.

Business Risks

A business risk is one that provides an opportunity for gain as well as for loss. An example of a business risk is a customer change to the project's scope. The change might represent a risk to the provider because it involves skills or expertise the company does not possess. However, the scope change might produce additional revenue if the company can hire additional resources, team with another company, or hire a vendor to provide the necessary expertise. Business risks are the risks that are managed. Management of insurable, or pure, risks should never be attempted.

Insurable or Pure Risks

Insurable risks, sometimes called pure risks because they offer only opportunities for loss, are risks that the organization should never take on. Incredibly, software development groups routinely attempt such projects because of the prevailing view that everything can be fixed with software.

Some examples of insurable risks are natural disasters such as fire, flood, hurricanes, and earthquakes. For instance, if a company is located in a high-risk area for hurricanes, it will insure against such loss. But there are other, more subtle types of pure risk. Often a company will attempt a project because the major project requirements are within the company's capability, even though one or two other requirements may not be. Because they are qualified to accomplish the majority of a project's requirements, they think that they will be able to complete the rest. Mature, or learning, organizations recognize these disastrous situations and plan for them. These organizations have effective project selection and risk management processes. The risk management process is best understood with the consideration of a risk management model such as the one that follows. This risk management model can be applied in any organization and for any industry.

Creating a Risk Management Model

Risk management, like every critical management activity, is best accomplished when a formalized and documented set of guidelines and standard operating procedures are implemented and followed by everyone in the company. The Project Management Institute (PMI®) has provided guidelines for a risk management process in its *Guide to the Project Management Body of Knowledge* (*PMBOK® Guide*), including their own model. The model in Exhibit 13-6 contains all the PMI® model steps but is more detailed to better explain

Exhibit 13-6. Risk management model.

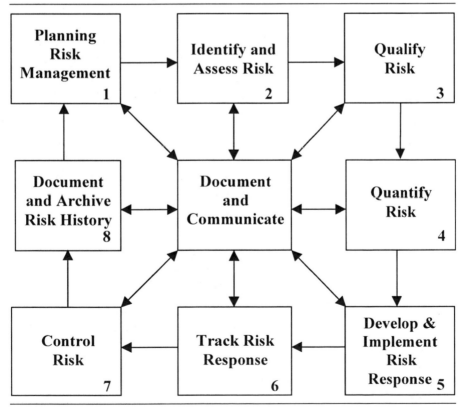

the risk management components and process elements. One key component of PMI's model that is implicit, but not stated, is that of continual evaluation. Risk management is an ongoing process that continues throughout the project's life cycle.

Planning Risk Management—The First Step

Risk planning should begin during the project selection phase. Project selection is the process of determining whether the company or organization should pursue a project. One criterion in the selection process is risk—risk in the schedule, budget, resources available, expertise required, and fit with the organization's strategic plan.

The major inputs to the risk-planning step are:

- The project charter
- Organizational policies or guidelines
- Contract documents (if the project results from an external customer; statement of work or other departmental project document if it is for an internal customer)
- The work breakdown structure (WBS)
- Network analysis

The project charter describes the project manager's limits of authority, the project priority, and support requirements from various functional units in the organization. The project charter readily identifies many potential risk areas. For instance, if the project priority is four, then it is immediately apparent that the project can lose out if resources are tight. Other risks are not always as obvious. In fact, these risks may be so subtle that if a project fails, they are never recognized. Consider, for example, a typical scenario in the IT environment: A project has the potential for propelling the organization into the next level of market competitiveness, if it is successful. Under this scenario, this type of project gets a great deal of senior-level scrutiny and guidance. It gets so much guidance, in fact, that senior management's good intentions can hamper the project manager's efforts to the point of project failure. In other words, too much of even a good thing can interject risk into the project. Only a good project sponsor, charter, and mature senior management can prevent this kind of risk from occurring.

Along with the project charter, there are other company policies and guidelines to aid the project team. These policies and guidelines include templates, checklists, and guidance for identifying and planning risk contingencies.

Contractual documents, particularly those from external customers, contain information that can usually identify potential risk areas. This information has to be factored into the project planning. For instance, most contracts contain at least a high-level schedule. If a customer has a hard schedule completion date requirement, it may represent a potential risk to the seller, if resources are insufficient to meet the date.

The WBS is the most important tool for risk planning because it contains all the project tasks, and, consequently, a quick view of the potential risks. Since tasks drive the skill set and resource requirements, it will be apparent whether the project requires effort that falls outside the organization's capability—a critical risk that requires either an alternative approach or a strategy to include teaming or outsourcing the work.

The network analysis provides insight into task interrelationships and potential risks associated with timing requirements and path convergence problems. Path convergence is the convergence of two or more network paths into a single node, as shown in Exhibit 13-7. In the exhibit, the convergence of paths from Tasks A, B, and C into Task D create greater uncertainties in starting the path out of D on time. If either of the durations for A, B, or C are in error, then the start time for D is affected. If all three are in error, then the start time of D is affected exponentially.

The major output of the risk-planning step is the risk management plan. The risk plan is part of the overall project management plan and is often provided as an attachment. Many customers, particularly public-sector customers, require a risk management plan as part of any proposal submitted on a competitive bid. Exhibit 13-8 is a sample risk management plan.

Exhibit 13-7. Path convergence in a network analysis.

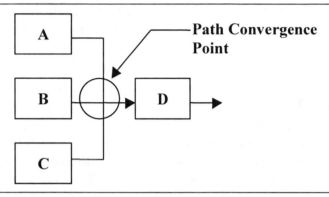

Exhibit 13-8. Risk management plan format.

Risk Management Plan

I.   Project name and brief scope description

II.   Risk management methodology

III. Roles and responsibilities

IV.   Funding

V.   Risk measurement and interpretation methodology

VI.   Levels of risk response responsibility

VII. Risk communication plan

VIII. Risk tracking and documentation

IX.   Appendixes
      i. Risk table
      ii. Risk response plan

Sections of the Risk Management Plan

The risk management plan guides you in the process of managing the risks of a particular project. Therefore, it is imperative that a plan is developed for every project and that the plan clearly identifies how the project risks will be identified, responded to, tracked, and controlled. Let us look at the nine sections of the risk management plan.

1. *Project Name and Brief Scope Description.* This section provides the name of the project (and often the project manager's name) as well as a short description of the project's purpose.

2. *Risk Management Methodology.* This section provides a narrative about the tools or techniques used to identify the risks and how the risk response strategies will be determined. This section also contains the data sources from which the risk and risk strategies are developed, such as historical data from previous, similar projects.

3. *Roles and Responsibilities.* The roles and responsibilities of each project team member and other task contributors should be clearly defined in this section. If responsibility to report, eliminate, or track a risk is not clearly assigned, even a usually diligent team member can easily ignore an impending risk event. Of course, the project manager has ultimate responsibility for administering the risk plan and risk response strategies, but he or she can, and should, delegate responsibility for identifying risks and reporting triggers that presage a risk event.

4. *Funding.* Budgets for risk contingencies should be defined and guidance for their administration published at the start of the project. Many organizations assign the responsibility for the contingency, or reserve funding, pool to the project manager. However, funding for contingencies is strictly the responsibility of senior management in other organizations. This section of the risk management plan should clearly state how the contingency funding is to be administered.

5. *Risk Measurement and Interpretation Methodology.* The method or methods used to measure risk and how the scores are interpreted are defined in this section. Most companies have guidelines for applying a weighting factor and/or a score for each type of risk. Scoring methods are important in both the quantitative and qualitative analyses to reduce the effects of subjectively assigning a value to a risk. Scoring methods should be chosen in advance, and

they should be applied consistently throughout all steps of the risk management process.

6. *Levels of Risk Response Responsibility.* This section defines who has responsibility for each risk response according to a predetermined threshold. That is, during a project's life cycle, risk events of different levels of impact can occur. The project manager has discretionary authority to handle certain levels of risk, but he or she must elevate the decision to a higher senior management position or to a committee, if the impact of the risk exceeds a certain monetary level. In some instances, only the customer has the authority to implement certain risk response strategies because of the cost to the project in time and money. The effectiveness of a risk management plan is measured against how well any actual risk event is kept below the lowest risk threshold.

7. *Risk Communication Plan.* This section describes report formats and outlines who receives reports of risk events, responses implemented, and the effectiveness of the risk response strategies.

8. *Risk Tracking and Documentation.* This section describes the process for tracking the effectiveness of the risk response strategies and how they are documented and archived as lessons learned.

9. *Appendixes.* This section provides a vehicle for attaching any additional information or plans, depending on the needs of each individual project. The two most common appendixes are the risk table and the risk response plan.

- *The Risk Table.* This is a table or matrix of all the identified risks in the project. Many project teams prefer that the table contains only those risks being managed at the moment and that it be changed or revised as you deal with each risk.
- *The Risk Response Plan.* This is a detailed plan explaining the response strategies for each of the identified risks in the risk table.

Identifying and Assessing Risks—The Second Step

Identifying risk is not a task that many project teams or organizations have done well in the past. Even today, risk identification and assessment, or the lack of it, is one of the key reasons that projects fail. In general, risk identification and risk management in general are not done well because of the difficulty in identifying risks. Given that risk is an uncertain and sometimes an unknown event, risk management tends to be viewed as more esoteric compared with the hard engineering components of the project. Therefore, many project teams and organizations are not comfortable with it. Once a procedure for identifying risks is in place, however, managing them becomes less scary and much easier.

Risk identification is best accomplished with a team simply because the collective knowledge and experience of a group of people is far greater than an individual's can be. There are several methods useful in the process, but the best methods all are some variation of brainstorming. The brainstorming technique itself is generally the one method that yields the greatest number of identified risks because it is designed to produce a large amount of data in a relatively short period of time.

Qualifying Risks—The Third Step

Qualifying risks involves three components or substeps—filtering the risk to determine if it actually is a risk and when it is likely to occur during the project's life cycle, determining the probability that a risk event will occur, and prioritizing the risk.

Filtering Risk

Once a list is developed, each risk is filtered to determine whether it is within the project's scope, if it is likely to occur, what its significance is, when it might occur within the project's life cycle, and even if it is a real risk. It is not uncommon to identify a potential risk only to decide after careful deliberation that it is not a risk at all, or, if it is a risk, that the consequences of the impact are so small as to not be a concern. The best method for assessing risks is through a process of filtering, such as the one shown in Exhibit 13-9. It is important not to prioritize risks at this stage. At this point of the analysis, the objective is to determine risk characteristics.

Many times a perceived risk is often not a risk when measured

Exhibit 13-9. The risk-filtering process.

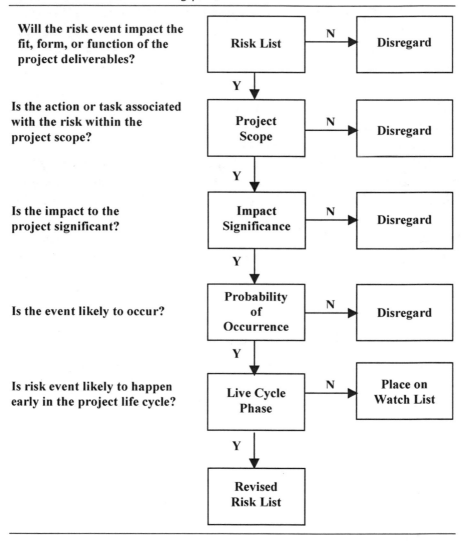

against the project's scope—if the action generating the perceived risk is not within the scope, then it is not a risk and can be ignored.

Filtering the list developed during risk identification results in a final or revised risk list. The next step is to determine the probability of risk event occurrence. Whenever possible, it is better to assign a percentage probability to the risk. This is because the next step of the risk analysis process is to quantify the risk or measure the relative importance of one risk over another.

It is not always possible to assign a percentage probability be-cause of the lack of historical data or experience. In those cases, the best that can be done is to assign a low, medium, or high proba-bility. Even in that case, a range of numerical values may be possi-ble, as shown in Exhibit 13-10. Even taking the middle of the range, or being pessimistic and taking the high end of the range, provides a numerical result for a better comparison. The impor-tance of assigning a percentage probability to the risk will become clear in the discussion on quantifying risks.

Prioritizing Risk

The risk-filtering step should result in a revised list of risks that accurately represent the most likely risk events to expect during a project's life cycle. Although it is important to identify potential risks, it is absolutely crucial to prioritize them. One serious mis-take that project managers make is to attempt to manage all the risks on the revised list. Fortunately, that is not necessary, because the reality is that we can manage about ten risks at a time.

Hence, for greater efficiency and effectiveness, a list of the top

Exhibit 13-10. Changing subjective ratings into percentages.

Risk	Very Low 0–5%	Low 6–15%	Medium 16–40%	High 41–80%	Very High 81–100%

ten risks should be actively managed with a watch list of the re-
mainder to replace those that are mitigated, controlled, eliminated,
or that do not materialize.

Quantifying Risks—The Fourth Step

Assigning a percentage value for risk probability creates opportunities for risk comparisons that would not otherwise exist. The
most difficult task throughout a risk analysis is estimating the
probability of occurrence of the event with any degree of accuracy.
One can argue that assigning a percentage of probability is very
subjective and, therefore, inaccurate. However, it must be remem-
bered that risks do not have to be measured in absolute terms to
be of value; they can be measured relative to each other.

The most commonly used tool for determining the relative
value of project risks is expected value. Expected value (EV) is a
technique useful in assessing different technical approaches or
making trade-off analyses. The concept is based on the probability
of different outcomes occurring, which explicitly considers the
risk of the different approaches. That is, if there is a chance that
one of several outcomes for a given scenario can occur depending
on the risks involved for each of the different conditions, then the
most likely outcome over time can be determined. This most likely
result is known as the expected value.

Expected value is based on the notion that each result is mutually exclusive. That is, the outcome is a random occurrence. A
probability can be assigned to that outcome. Mathematically, expected value can be defined in this fashion. Suppose a random variable X, defined if the set of its possible values is given and if the
probability of each value's appearance is also given, possesses n
values. Then, these possible values can be represented as X_1, X_2,
. . . X_n

If p_1, p_2, . . . p_n are the probabilities associated with each X,
then the *expected value* of X can be represented by the equation:

$$EV = \sum_{i=0}^{n} p_i X_i$$

The interpretation of this equation is that the expected value of an event is the sum of all the possible values of the variable, multiplied by the probability of each of those values occurring. The key point about expected value is that it is most effective when it is used to compare two or more potential outcomes, which helps eliminate some of the subjectivity in a risk analysis. An example will demonstrate how expected value is used.

Example

Would you spend $100 for the chance to win $1,000 if the three possibilities of taking this chance are as shown in the table?

Event Possibilities (Xp)	Amount to Win the Event (p)	Probability of Expected Value (p)	
1	0	60%	0
2	$200	30%	$60
3	$1,000	10%	$100
		Total EV =	$160

The sum of the expected values for this example is $160, which is interpreted as the likely result of this investment, not a bad return on the investment of $100. But it is also important to analyze the worse and best cases—how much you could lose and how much you can win. In this example, expected analysis indicates that you will make at least $60 on the investment, but that just indicates the most likely outcome—you could win $1,000, but you could lose everything. A risk-averse person wouldn't take the chance at all; a risk taker would.

Developing and Implementing Risk Response Strategies—The Fifth Step

Risk response strategies are the project manager's methods for managing the risk events that occur. A proactive approach to risk management, as with every facet of project management, lessens the impact of those risks that can be identified early in the project's life cycle. There are also response strategies to maximize potential opportunities generated by risk events. Generally, there are three techniques for responding to negative risks, or threats: avoidance, transference, and mitigation.

Avoiding Risk

Often the best defense against a risk event is simply to avoid it. We know that risks occur in every project, and it is not feasible, or wise, to try to structure a project to have no risks. A project without risk is not worth pursuing. On the other hand, facing a risk that is likely to end in loss of time, revenues, or even the entire project is also unwise. It is unwise also to accept a risk that we have defined as a pure or insurable risk. In these cases, it is best to consider alternative approaches that allow the risk to be transferred, or lacking that, avoided altogether.

The most common way of avoiding a risk is to consider an alternative approach that contains less or no risk. For example, if a system design calls for a new, undeveloped software operating system, it could represent a significant risk to the project. A less risky approach would be to use a proven off-the-shelf operating system, provided that it meets the customer's requirements. A common occurrence in IT projects occurs during the development of a system that has a specified operating system for which a new version is developed prior to system completion. If the new software version is likely to have defects, it could be better to avoid any attendant risks by continuing with the previous version.

Transferring Risk

Risk transference is commonly done in practice by teaming or by hiring a vendor. When the project requires expertise not resident in the organization or group, it is common practice to team with another company or to hire a vendor who does possess the requisite expertise. Common examples of risk transference also occur where insurance is the practical way of planning for risks. For instance, a company that is located in a flood plain or in a tornado alley would routinely purchase insurance against such risks.

Mitigating Risk

Mitigating risk means that the risk event is controlled in such a way that either the impact or the probability of the event occurrence is lessened. Mitigation can occur either by reducing the level of impact, that is, cost or schedule added to the baseline, or by reducing the probability of the event occurring, or both. Generally, mitigation occurs by adding more resources or by using better-trained or more experienced personnel. Using tested and tried technology rather than newer, untested technology can also mitigate risk. Risk mitigation is a form of risk acceptance. That is, the risk is expected, and it is an acceptable risk to take; however, an attempt is made to significantly reduce the impact to the project.

There are three response strategies for dealing with risk having potentially positive impacts on a project's objectives: exploit, share, and enhance.

Exploiting Positive Risks

This strategy seeks to eliminate the uncertainty associated with a particular positive risk by making the opportunity happen. One way to exploit responses is to assign more talented, or experienced, people to the project to reduce project time to completion, or to significantly improve the quality of the product beyond that originally planned.

Sharing Positive Risks

Sharing a positive risk involves a third party: risk-sharing partnerships, special purpose teams, or even companies or joint ventures. Sharing positive risks could be as simple as involving a vendor, or a consultant, with specialized expertise.

Enhancing Positive Risks

This strategy seeks to modify the size of an opportunity by increasing the probability that the event will happen and by increasing the impact if it does.

Developing a Response Strategy for Both Negative and Positive Risks

Risk acceptance is simply that—the risk is expected, and the level of impact to the project is within the tolerance level of the project team or organization. Usually, this kind of risk is the result of things such as the unpredictability of resource availability. For example, there is always a certain level of risk associated with the real-world problem of sharing resources across multiple projects. A risk to the schedule exists if the resources are not available at the time they are needed. In such cases, the risk, negative or positive, is recognized and accepted, and it will be dealt with when it occurs.

Implementing Risk Response Strategies

Once a course of action has been developed for a risk event, the strategy must be implemented. A good strategy includes risk triggers to alert the project team of impending risk events. Although the project manager has the ultimate responsibility for the risk plan, he or she may designate team members to monitor risk events likely to occur in their technical areas. Monitoring risks involves more than observing whether the anticipated risks occur; it involves determining if the strategies to respond to the risks are adequate or whether other actions are required, which is a function of the next step: tracking risk response.

Tracking Risk Response—The Sixth Step

Tracking risk response is the process of determining whether the planned response strategy is working or whether an alternative approach is needed. It also involves determining if new, unidentified risks occur as a result of implementing response strategies and if the project assumptions are still valid. As a result of risk response tracking, the project may need to be replanned, particularly if the response strategies are not effective or the original assumptions are not valid.

Controlling Risk—The Seventh Step

Risks are controlled in one of two ways: contingency plans and workaround actions. Contingency plans are plans for implementing risk response strategies. These are plans that can be developed when a potential risk event is identified. Most project risks fall into the category of identifiable risks and are controllable through contingency planning.

Contingency planning usually involves setting aside some level of reserve, usually money but occasionally time as well, to ensure the project is kept on schedule. For example, if a risk is that some critical resources might not be available when needed, the contingency might be to hire a vendor or technical consultants to fill the resource void. Contingencies nearly always require additional funding—hence the need for a contingency reserve.

Workaround actions are activities implemented when the risk could not be foreseen or planned for. These events almost always cost more than the project budget originally allowed, so the funding is taken from a management reserve. Both contingency and management reserves are established specifically to ensure that the project is kept on schedule if a risk event occurs. The basic difference between the two types of reserve is that contingencies are planned into the project budget and are usually controlled by the project manager, whereas the management reserve is not a part of the project budget and is controlled by senior management.

Documenting and Archiving Risk History—The Eighth Step

Neither project managers nor organizations are careful enough about documenting lessons-learned and archiving them so that future projects can reap the benefits. The most common excuse is that the team members from a closing project are needed to start new projects and cannot be spared for lessons-learned meetings. Ironically, meetings to develop lessons-learned-information usually do not take much time since the information, in the form of status reports, audits, and other project paperwork, already contains the pertinent information. Lessons-learned meetings generally take between two hours and a few days, depending on the size and complexity of the project. If the project manager and team members have maintained a complete project file, the lessons-learned information is already available—all that is needed is compilation of the information into a lessons-learned binder. The basic lessons-learned file information includes:

- Project name and start and finish date
- Key stakeholders, such as the project manager, sponsor, task leaders, and customer
- Baseline and actual budget and schedule charts
- Project issues and their resolution
- Identified risks and results of contingency plans
- Unidentified risks, their resolution, and project impact
- Analysis of team planning and performance
- Analysis of metrics collection and usage
- Analysis of what went right and what went wrong in the project

Every lessons-learned analysis should be documented and archived with easy access given to all project managers and teams. Many companies have begun making these lessons-learned libraries available online to make them even more accessible and effective. But even a hard copy in the organization's resource library is far better than no access at all. Many projects have been saved the problems and costs of reinventing the wheel by having access to workable solutions for risks that continue to reoccur.

Summary

The implementation phase of a project's life cycle involves starting the project, monitoring its progress, and controlling day-to-day activities so that variances from the project plan are kept to a minimum.

The key to success in this phase is monitoring the system design. If the project manager and team put into place a systematic way to collect data, analyze the data, control the variances revealed in the analyses, and report the results quickly, then the project will progress smoothly. Otherwise, the project will be characterized by constant, reactive attempts to put out fires.

Another key aspect of project success revolves around the expertise and efficiency of the team in risk management. Amazingly, a large segment of the corporate world does not engage in any formalized risk planning process. Not to do so is to invite disaster.

The key tools for this phase of the project are the WBS, Gantt charts, network analyses, earned value analyses, statistical analyses, and various report formats.

CHAPTER 14

The Termination Phase

Do not turn back when you are just at the goal.

—PUBLILIUS SYRUS
Maxims

One characteristic of a project is that it is of temporary duration. By definition, every project has a definite ending point. The problem is that projects have a definite ending point only if there is a formal ending to the project. Otherwise, projects can extend beyond what would normally be considered the ending point, even for years beyond. In my seminars, I often have students ask, "How do you get a project to end?" or say, "I have a project that never seems to go away."

The termination phase is as important as any other phase, but many organizations do not support the activities of this phase because of the competitive pressure to start other projects even as the current project is winding down. Nevertheless, the project manager needs to focus on the termination phase with the same intensity as, or maybe more than, the other phases.

Terminating a project is one of the most important, and often one of the most difficult, phases of the project's life cycle. The problem is that when the project approaches the end, the team members begin looking for their next assignment, and they lose interest in the project they are working on. Also, functional managers begin to siphon off team members and assign them to other projects. The net result is that the project manager is often faced with the task of bringing the project to closure, but with virtually no resources.

To preclude some of the problems encountered during project closure, the project manager should begin planning for the termination phase at the beginning of the project. Project managers who focus on the one goal of delivering the end item to the customer are too narrow in their perspective and fail to define other, equally important goals—goals that should be part and parcel of every project in the organization. Exhibit 14-1 lists the general goals of every project manager during the termination phase of a new project. Naturally, this list is not inclusive. Each project will have to be tailored to the organization's goals, and each project manager and team will also have several personal goals to strive for.

One can make the argument that the goals in Exhibit 14-1 are nothing more than what the project manager should be doing anyway as a part of the job, and that is absolutely correct. The problem is that not every project manager or organization will worry about anything much beyond items 1 and 2 unless they are adopted as formal goals of the project.

Why Projects End

Projects end for essentially three reasons:

1. The project goals and objectives are met.
2. The benefits or original reasons for the project no longer are viable.
3. The contractor defaults on the project.

Clearly, the number one reason is the most desirable reason of them all. The objective always is to terminate the project after all the requirements are met and to do it in a planned, disciplined, and orderly fashion. The steps in achieving this planned, disciplined, and orderly termination will be discussed later in this chapter.

Exhibit 14-1. The general project termination goals of every project manager.

- Provide the customer with the product or service specified.
- Strive to meet the project goals on time and on budget.
- Maintain open communications with all stakeholders.
- Request and support at least two audits during the project life cycle.
- Document and file in the organization's library a complete history of the project.
- Document lessons learned for the project.
- Actively seek new positions for the project team members.

The second reason for termination is by far the most difficult one—difficult in terms of coming to grips with the necessity and advisability of terminating the project and then acting on it. (This is not the most damaging reason for termination, but it is the most difficult one.) These are the projects that had good goals and objectives and might even have been managed efficiently and effectively. There may not be anything inherently wrong with these projects except that they are no longer relevant to the organization's or customer's overall strategic or business goals. Project managers and their organizations just do not like to terminate a project once it gets started and before it is completed. Perhaps they view such a termination as a failure, but rather than a failure, evaluating the efficacy of a project periodically and deciding whether it should continue is a sound business practice.

Every project, especially those that are for internal customers, should have go/no-go decision points to provide senior management with an opportunity to reassess the project as it reaches predetermined milestones and make a decision whether it is beneficial to continue.

Suppose senior management decides to pursue a new line of business, one significantly different from the organization's usual business endeavors. The project manager for this effort has been given a budget to modernize, change, or buy new equipment as appropriate, hire the requisite skills, and begin producing the product. However, because this new business line is so different, the planners underestimated the start-up costs. Now that the project is under way and the project team is more sophisticated about the real requirements and costs, the project manager can present the senior executives with a more realistic estimate of the costs for getting into this new market area.

The benefits may far outweigh the costs in this scenario, making it worth the additional expense to continue with the project. But suppose senior management discovers that they may not be able to capitalize their investment. What should the company do? The answer seems patently clear: Cut the losses and terminate the project. Coming to that conclusion and making that decision can be excruciating, and many organizations will continue to pour money into that hole before they can accept that it just does not make any sense to continue with the project.

Sometimes the customer makes the decision that the project should not continue. This decision, especially if from an external customer, can be devastating to the contractor. Even if the customer is happy with the work of the contractor, the perception often exists that the project was terminated because the contractor did not perform up to expectations. In addition, having the project terminated, even on good terms, means having a project team without assigned or billable work.

The third category for terminating a project is by far the worst. When a contractor defaults or the customer has to terminate for cause, that means the contractor did not perform technically—in short, it could not or did not produce. Being terminated because of the inability to perform technically damages the company's reputation and demoralizes employees.

Project Management Activities During the Termination Phase

The primary responsibility of the project manager is to ensure that all work on the project has been completed. But completing the project is only a small part of the work that has to be accomplished in this phase. Exhibit 14-2 provides a checklist of the major activities that need to be accomplished in the termination phase.

Exhibit 14-2. Project manager's checklist of termination activities.

1. Customer
   - Deliver end item.
   - Install and test end item.
   - Review project scope with customer.
   - Obtain formal acceptance from customer.

2. Project Organization
   - Recognize and reward project team members.
   - Reassign project personnel.
   - Provide personnel reports and recommendations to functional managers.

3. Financial
   - Submit final invoice to customer.
   - Submit final payments to vendors.
   - Close all project charge codes.

4. Site/Equipment
   - Close project site.
   - Dispose of equipment and furniture.

Activities with the Customer at Termination

If a project manager establishes a close working relationship with the customer, as should be the case, then getting to final closure on the end item should not be too difficult. Acceptance of the end item by the customer should be virtually a formality if the project manager and customer have monitored the project closely, talked about and resolved any discrepancies as they occurred, and had agreement on the project's goals and objectives in the first place.

One difficulty at this stage is in making sure that all the deliverables are turned over to the customer and that all are accepted. For instance, most products, and sometimes services, require supporting documentation, such as operating or training manuals. Sometimes, one of the deliverables will be a support plan or the initial stock of spare parts. The point is that the project manager has to view the project as a system and ensure that everything is accounted for.

Many projects often require installation and testing. It is not uncommon for the customer to withhold some percentage of the contract price, say 10 percent, until the installation, testing, and, occasionally, some period of operation are completed. Only then, when the customer is completely satisfied that the product delivered is the product contracted for, will the final payment be made and the contract closed. All these contractual requirements have to be planned for at the beginning of the project so that they can be dealt with at the project's closeout.

Another difficulty in the termination phase is the amount of paperwork required and the effort needed to ensure that it is all completed. We will discuss the different reports that have to be accomplished as each of the major termination activities is addressed.

Organizational Activities

Project termination is usually an emotional time for the project team. Sometimes it can be depressing. If team members are hired solely for that project, project termination can mean that some team members will be laid off. But even without the specter of a layoff, team members will be anxious about what their next job is, causing disruption.

One of the great ironies in project management is that if a project manager gets complete team member buy-in at the front end of the project, which is what we all strive for, it can backfire as the project approaches termination. The reality is that if team members become too attached to the project, they sometimes will sabotage it to prevent it from ending—and at the very time the project manager needs complete teamwork to close the project and make the schedule.

The termination phase is also the phase during which personality problems emerge as a major source of conflict.[1] This really is not surprising, since it is during this period that the interesting project work is completed, and team members are either being siphoned off for other projects or are worrying about their new assignment—even whether there will be a new assignment. The project manager has to be sensitive to these problems and try to keep the team focused on finishing the requirements.

Although the project manager has no functional authority over project personnel, he or she should make every reasonable effort to facilitate reassignment to other projects as each individual's work is finished. There are two reasons why trying to get team members reassigned should be a priority with the project manager: It is the right thing to do, and it will pay enormous dividends for both the project manager and the organization in the future.

Helping team members get reassigned after project termination is the right thing to do because they have, after all, dedicated themselves to the successful accomplishment of the project. Without the team and team member support, the project manager would never accomplish the project goals and objectives. And the best reward for any employee is a demonstration that his or her work is appreciated and valued. Finding new work for these employees in the organization is the highest form of flattery.

The second reason for helping team members find new assignments is a little self-serving but important nonetheless. Helping to find new jobs for the team reflects well on the project manager and the organization. The team members will respond with loyalty and support. The old unwritten contract between employee and employer—if an employee worked hard and was loyal to the company, he or she would have a job for life—no longer exists. That feeling of trust between employer and employee needs to be rebuilt; helping the team member find a new job within the organization is a step in that direction.

One of the reports that the project manager will submit during termination is a personnel report. Since the project manager has no functional authority over team personnel, he or she does not write performance reviews. However, the project manager is often asked to make inputs for an individual's performance review because the project manager has observed the individual's work and team behavior at close hand. In the same vein, the project manager should submit a personnel report to all the appropriate functional managers, detailing each individual's work ethic, team skills, technical expertise, and whether the person should be assigned to future projects. This report should have limited and confidential distribution.

Financial Activities

Getting paid for the project work is a significant milestone in any project, and is, of course, the reason why the company is in business. But there are other financial matters that have to be attended to as well.

Almost every project will have vendors supporting it. The project manager has to ensure that all vendors are notified that the project is closing and that all outstanding invoices have to be submitted. The project manager also has to close all charge codes used in the project by notifying the accounting department and all functional groups in the company that no charges against the project will be accepted after a given date.

Site and Equipment Closeout

Many projects are executed on-site, which means that the contractor performs on the project at the customer's location. Often the customer provides office or work space for the project, but usually on-site means that the contractor has to lease office and work space within a specified radius of the customer's location. If the project is accomplished on the customer's premises, there may not be much site-closing activity required beyond the removal of personal belongings and company equipment. In the latter case, the project manager will have to close out the lease, stop all utilities, disconnect telephone service, and notify all suppliers. In either case, the project manager is responsible for packing and shipping the company-owned supplies and equipment back to the parent company.

Often, particularly with government contracts, the customer will furnish equipment to the contractor to accomplish the job. For instance, it is common for a customer to furnish special test equipment or special tools to a project. It is also common for the customer to furnish computers to a project, particularly if the project is to develop some type of computer-based training. The customer provides the computers so that the software can be developed, loaded, and tested on the computer before shipment to the customer. In each case, the equipment provided for the project still belongs to the customer and must be accounted for and returned to the customer at the end of the contract. (A special case of customer-furnished equipment is when the customer has excess equipment or parts and provides them to the contractor as a cheaper alternative than manufacturing them anew.)

Project Auditing

One of the final tasks of the project team is to perform a complete evaluation of the project. This task is often overlooked, but it is essential that every project, regardless of how the project ended, be evaluated for lessons learned. Unless there is a formal review, the tendency is to mentally suppress problems encountered and to understate the impact of past errors or misjudgments.[2] In short, we convince ourselves that things weren't really so bad after all.

Some authors refer to this stage as *evaluation* or *summary evaluation*. However, the project manager should consider this an audit because the word *audit* implies a more disciplined approach, greater detail, and a look at every aspect of the project, which is what is needed and expected by the stakeholders.

The problem with any evaluation of work done is that there is a tendency to explain away or gloss over things that went wrong or to point fingers and lay blame for problems. Project evaluations are not to fix blame but to review the performance of the team and the project end item. Making this evaluation a formal one tends to result in a more objective evaluation and with data that is more useful to the organization.

There should be a true audit of the project midway through the schedule as well as at the end. These audits are best done by an independent team of experts as opposed to the project team performing it. The reason for an independent audit team is, of course, to get around the problems previously mentioned. An independent audit team can encounter other and quite different problems, such as:

- Resentment by the project team
- Fear that the audit team will uncover problems (hence, the project team is not forthcoming with information)

- Disruption to the project
- Less understanding of the project's goals and objectives, and thus biased conclusions
- Fear by the project team that the auditors will place blame for problems

The project manager has to be sensitive to these problems and work to mitigate the project team's fears and facilitate a quick and accurate audit. One way to do this is to include on the audit team people who are known to and respected by the project team. It is not uncommon to request that a senior member of the project team be a part of the audit process, a solution that offers two major benefits: It serves to calm the project team, and it is a way for the audit team to reach more accurate conclusions by having someone intimately familiar with the project interpret the project goals, objectives, and requirements.

The audit team composition is critical to the success of the audit process. It is usually my recommendation that someone other than the project manager—perhaps the project manager's supervisor—organize the team. The size of the audit team is generally a function of the size of the project: a large, complex project requires a larger audit team to evaluate it. Audit team members can be drawn from a variety of areas, but all should have expertise in some aspect of the project. Some of the areas from which team members can be recruited are:

- Contracts
- Marketing
- Finance or accounting
- Human resources
- Technical functional groups
- Facilities
- Logistics

Whatever the makeup of the audit team, the members have to approach the evaluation with complete objectivity. It is their job to evaluate the performance of the project team, including the project manager, and the performance of the project.

The audit report contains an assessment of every aspect of the project. Exhibit 14-3 is a format that can be used as a guide to writing the report. Clearly, not every project will require a format as complete as this one. Each project will have more or fewer elements than are represented in the exhibit. But in general, it is helpful to have a format available, and companies that support the audit process will usually have a standard format as a part of their operating procedures.

The project manager should also remember that the audit report is a communication tool. Therefore, it is his or her responsibility to prepare a distribution list for the document. Again, if the organization has a standard audit format, then it will likely have a minimum distribution list as well.

As a word of caution, there are two things that should never happen. First, the audit report should be prepared in a professional manner and never contain derogatory remarks about individuals. Any assessments of an individual's behavior or performance should be documented but should have limited and confidential distribution. Second, the project manager should never allow senior management to be blindsided. If there are problems that the project manager knows will surface in an audit report, the appropriate senior management should be advised about them before they are read in the final audit report.

Summary

The termination phase of the project's life cycle is as important as any other phase, yet many project managers and their organizations do not place as much value on this phase as it deserves. The primary reason for this is that any organization that is basically project-oriented and, especially, dependent on external contracts for their core business is under enormous competitive pressure to move on to new projects as quickly as possible. This usually means that functional managers start reassigning project team members to new projects even before their old assignment is completed.

Exhibit 14-3. Example format for a final project audit report.

Project Audit Report for _____

I.   Executive Summary
II.   Introduction
III.   Project Review
    A. Project objectives
    B. Methodology or approach
IV.   Planning Effectiveness
V.   Project Management Effectiveness
VI.   Effectiveness of Technical Solution
VII.   Project Deliverables
    A. Description
    B. Assessment against requirements
VIII.   Quality
    A. Standards used
    B. Measuring
    C. Assessment against requirements
IX.   Schedule
    A. Delays
       1. Reasons
       2. Recovery actions
    B. Assessment against plan
X.   Resources Utilization
    A. Effectiveness
    B. Problems
       1. Reasons
       2. Recovery actions
XI.   Resources Utilization
    A. Effectiveness
    B. Problems
       1. Reasons
       2. Recovery actions
XII.   Individual Team Member Assessment and Recommendations (submit as separate, confidential report)
XIII.   Lessons Learned
XIV.   Recommendations

The project manager must plan for the termination phase well in advance of the scheduled project end—ideally in the development phase of the project's life cycle. And the project manager must resist, within realistic bounds, the siphoning off of team members prior to a formal project termination date. Although this is not easy to do since the project manager does not have functional authority over the team members, one thing that can help is to include the termination requirements and responsibilities in the project's charter.

Although the primary emphasis in any project is to provide the end product to the customer on time and on schedule, the project manager must not forget that there are ancillary support items required in each project. For instance, almost every project requires documentation such as operating manuals. The project manager has to ensure that all requirements of the project are satisfied.

Finally, one important task in the termination phase that is often overlooked is the final audit or evaluation. This important task is critical to the organization because it is from these audits that future projects can be made better. The audit is accomplished principally for the lessons learned that can be applied to future projects.

Endnotes

Chapter 1

1. *A Guide to the Project Management Body of Knowledge* (Newtown Square, PA: PMI, 2004).

2. Barry Z. Posner, "What It Takes to Be a Good Project Manager," *Project Management Journal* (March 1987).

Chapter 2

1. Claude Shannon and Warren Weaver, *The Mathematical Theory of Communication* (Urbana, IL: University of Illinois Press, 1949).

2. Deborah Dumaine, *Write to the Top: Writing for Corporate Success* (New York: Random House, 1989).

3. W. Strunk and E.B. White, *The Elements of Style,* 4th ed. (New York: Macmillan, 2000).

4. Beverly Davenport Sypher, Robert N. Bostrom, and Joy Hart Seibert, "Listening, Communication Abilities, and Success at Work," *Journal of Business Communication* (Fall 1989).

5. Clifton Fadiman, ed., *The Little, Brown Book of Anecdotes* (Boston: Little, Brown, 1985).

6. Thomas Leech, *How to Prepare, Stage, and Deliver Winning Presentations* (New York: AMACOM Books, 1982).

7. Colin Powell with Joseph E. Persico, *My American Journey* (New York: Random House, 1995).

Chapter 3

1. The following two books are especially helpful to project managers: Roger Fisher and William Ury, *Getting to Yes,* 2nd ed. (New York: Penguin Books, 1992), and David A. Lax and James K. Sebenius, *The Manager as Negotiator* (New York: Free Press, 1984).

2. H. J. Thamhain and D. L. Wilemon, "Conflict Management in Project Life Cycles," *Sloan Management Review* (Summer 1975).

3. The following books provide help on negotiating with vendors: James C. Freund, *Smart Negotiating: How to Make Good Deals in the Real World* (New York: Simon & Shuster, 1992); Howard Raiffa, *The Art and Science of Negotiation* (Cambridge, MA: Belknap Press of Harvard University Press, 1982); Max H. Bazerman and Margaret A. Neale, *Negotiating Rationally* (New York: Free Press, 1992).

4. J. Davidson Frame, *Managing Projects in Organizations*, rev. ed. (San Francisco: Jossey-Bass, 1995).

5. Fisher and Ury, *Getting to Yes.*

Chapter 4

1. W. G. Bennis and B. Nannus, *Leaders: The Strategies for Taking Charge* (New York: HarperBusiness Essentials, 2003).

2. Bernard M. Bass, *Bass and Stogdill's Handbook of Leadership,* 3rd ed. (New York: Free Press, 1990).

3. Ibid.

4. James M. Kouzes and Barry Z. Posner, *The Leadership Challenge,* 3rd ed. (San Francisco: Jossey-Bass, 1989).

5. Ibid.

Chapter 5

1. A. B. Badiru, *Project Management in Manufacturing and High Technology Operations* (New York: Wiley, 1988); S. F. Love, *Achieving Problem Free Project Management* (New York: Wiley, 1989).

Chapter 7

1. J. Davidson Frame, *The New Project Management* (San Francisco: Jossey-Bass, 1994).

Chapter 8

1. J. Davidson Frame, *The New Project Management* (San Francisco: Jossey-Bass, 2002).

2. For information about more sophisticated models, see Jack R. Meredith and Samuel J. Mantel, Jr., *Project Management: A Managerial Approach,* 5th ed (New York: Wiley, 2003) and Harold Kerzner, *Project Management: A Systems Approach to Planning, Scheduling, and Controlling,* 8th ed. (New York: Wiley, 2003).

3. For information about Emotional Intelligence, see Daniel Goleman, Richard Boyatzis, and Annie McKee, *Primal Leadership: Realizing the Power of Emotional Intelligence* (Boston: Harvard Business School Press, 2002) and Hendrie Weisinger, *Emotional Intelligence at Work* (San Francisco: Jossey-Bass, 1998).

Chapter 11

1. CIO/PMI Survey, *CIO Magazine,* July 1, 2003.

2. Gerard M. Hill, *The Complete Project Management Office Handbook* (Boca Raton, FL: Auerbach Publications, 2004).

Chapter 13

1. John M. Nicholas, *Managing Business and Engineering Projects: Concepts and Implementation* (Englewood Cliffs, NJ: Prentice Hall, 1990). Copyright © 1990. Reprinted by permission of Prentice-Hall, Inc., Upper Saddle River, N.J.

Chapter 14

1. H. J. Thamhain and D. L. Wilemon, "Conflict Management in Project Life Cycles," *Sloan Management Review* (Summer 1975).

2. John M. Nicholas, *Managing Business and Engineering Projects: Principles and Practice* (Oxford: Elsevier Butterworth-Heinemann, 2004).

Additional Resources of Interest

Ashby, Meredith D., and Stephen A. Miles. *Leaders Talk Leadership: Top Executives Speak Their Mind.* Oxford: Oxford University Press, 2002.

Bennis, Warren, Gretchen M. Spreitzer, and Thomas G. Cummings, eds. *The Future of Leadership: Today's Top Leadership Thinkers Speak of Tomorrow's Leaders.* San Francisco: Jossey-Bass, 2001.

Berger, Lance A., and Dorothy R. Berger. *The Talent Management Handbook: Creating Organizational Excellence by Identifying, Developing, and Promoting Your Best People.* New York: McGraw-Hill, 2003.

Breslin, William J., and Jeffrey Z. Rubin, eds. *Negotiation Theory and Practice.* Cambridge, MA: Harvard Law School, 1991.

Byham, William C., Audrey B. Smith, and Matthew J. Paese. *Grow Your Own Leaders: How to Identify, Develop, and Retain Leadership Talent.* New York: Financial Times Prentice Hall, 2002.

Frame, J. Davidson. *Managing Projects in Organizations,* 2nd ed. San Francisco: Jossey-Bass, 2002.

Fuller, George. *The Negotiator's Handbook.* Englewood Cliffs, NJ: Prentice Hall, 1991.

Kerzner, Harold. *Project Management: A Systems Approach to Planning, Scheduling, and Controlling,* 8th ed. New York: Wiley, 2003.

Lewicki, Roy J., Joseph A. Litterer, David M. Saunders, and John

W. Minton. *Negotiation: Readings, Exercises, and Cases,* 2d ed. Burr Ridge, IL: Richard C. Irwin, 1993.

Meredith, Jack R., and Samuel J. Mantel, Jr. *Project Management: A Managerial Approach,* 5th ed. New York: Wiley, 2003.

Ury, William. *Getting Past No: Negotiating Your Way From Confrontation to Cooperation.* New York: Bantam Books, 1993.

Young, H. Peyton, ed. *Negotiation Analysis.* Ann Arbor, MI: University of Michigan Press, 1991.

Yukl, Gary. *Leadership in Organizations.* New York: Prentice Hall, 2005.

Yukl, Gary, and Richard Lepsinger. *Flexible Leadership: Creating Value by Balancing Multiple Challenges and Choices.* New York: Pfeiffer Publishers, 2004.

Index

LaVergne, TN USA
15 December 2009
167114LV00005B/38/P